The Essential Slow Cooker Cookbook for Beginners

THE ESSENTIAL
SLOW COOKER
COOKBOOK
FOR BEGINNERS

100 Easy, Hands-Off Recipes for Your Slow Cooker

Pamela Ellgen

Photography by Tara Donne

ROCKRIDGE
PRESS

Interior and Cover Designer: Lindsey Dekker
Art Producer: Sara Feinstein
Editor: Kelly Koester
Production Editor: Rachel Taenzler
Production Manager: Riley Hoffman
Photography © 2021 Tara Donne. Food styling by Cyd McDowell

ISBN: Print 978-1-64876-861-3 | eBook 978-1-64876-862-0
R0

For Rich, the love of my life.

CONTENTS

Introduction

You bought your first slow cooker. Gasp! What now?

Don't worry, I've got you covered. With this book, you'll become a slow cooking master chef, and the slow cooker will become your favorite kitchen appliance.

I'll let you in on a little secret—cooking with a slow cooker is not very different from cooking in a pot on the stovetop. The key differences are that you don't need to tend to the food while it cooks and the food cooks much more slowly than it does on the stove. That's really it.

Okay, so there's a little more to it than that, which is why you have this book in your hands. I'll give you tips and tricks to make the most of your slow cooker, plus I'll show you which ingredients and types of dishes work best. Sure, you *can* make cookies in a slow cooker, but other foods, like Chocolate Lava Cake (page 113), were made for the slow cooker, so I'll be focusing on those.

Although I grew up on meals made in slow cookers, I didn't fall in love with slow cooking until I started surfing as an adult. After getting out of the cold waters of a November surf session, I didn't want to make dinner from scratch. I just wanted it to be ready on its own. The slow cooker made that possible (and it reined in my burgeoning restaurant budget).

Now slow cooking is my go-to cooking method for easy meals for my whole family, especially when we're juggling school, work, and of course, a quick dip in the ocean.

No matter what your skill level is in the kitchen, it's easy to learn how to use slow cookers to make comforting, family-friendly dishes from scratch.

I hope that this book is the start of many happy slow cooker memories to come.

CHAPTER 1

Going Slow Like a Pro

Welcome to the wonderful world of slow cooking! Before we get to the recipes, let's cover a few essentials. In this chapter, I'll share how slow cookers work, give you a guide to basic slow cooking, show you how to maximize your prep time, and teach you techniques for getting the most flavor out of your slow cooker meals. I'll also recommend essential pantry staples so that you have almost everything you need to cook any recipe in this book.

The Cooker That Never Goes Out of Style

Slow cookers have been used by home cooks all around the world for more than 70 years. Although food fads—and trendy appliances—come and go, home cooks have stuck by the slow cooker all these years because it is a culinary workhorse. Here are a few reasons slow cookers have stood the test of time.

Affordable. Although I adore fancy new cookware, I always balk at the high price tags. Slow cookers, on the other hand, usually cost less than $50, even for versions that come with some bells and whistles. There's no need to splurge on the top model to make the recipes in this book, though.

Easy-peasy. Slow cookers are pretty much foolproof. Just put the food in, cover the crock with a lid, turn it on, and wait. It doesn't get much easier than that.

Bold flavors. I'm a fan of cooking show competitions, and one of the ways the judges compliment chefs is by telling them their food tastes as if it cooked for a long time. That's because it takes time to develop flavor in food. Slow cookers have a way of coaxing the flavor out. You can build big, bold flavors out of very simple ingredients without hovering over the stove for hours.

Convenient. The convenience factor of slow cookers can't be beat. I love adding ingredients to the cooker in the morning, going to work, and coming home at the end of the day to a fully cooked meal that my whole family will love.

In this book, I focus on the dishes that work best in a slow cooker, such as roasts, braises, chilis, soups, stews, dips, and casseroles. By following some best practices for prep and cooking, which are outlined later in this chapter, anyone can create restaurant-quality dishes using a slow cooker.

Before we dive in, let's get a handle on what's going on inside the slow cooker while it's cooking.

How Slow Cookers Work

Slow cooker features vary from brand to brand, but they all operate basically the same way: a heating element keeps a lidded pot at a steady, even temperature for hours.

In most slow cooker models, the heating element is made up of bands of nickel or chrome wire that wrap around a fiberglass strip inside the cooker. This heats the stoneware or the metal crock. Throughout this book, I'll call the insert in the slow cooker the "slow cooker crock." This is important to keep in mind because when I call for coating the interior of the slow cooker crock with butter or oil, I'm definitely not talking about the heating element. That may seem obvious, but I just want to make sure we're on the same page before we get started.

As the slow cooker heats up, the lid helps distribute the heat from the walls of the crock to the food inside. As with stovetop cooking, the lid prevents steam from escaping, ensuring that the ingredients stay tender as they cook. In many models, placing the lid on the crock starts the cooking process. The slow cooker I use, however, is a little more pedestrian—you have to manually turn it on.

The heating element in most cookers is located in the lower third of the base, and a layer of insulation prevents hot spots from building, which is important because hot spots could burn your food. This feature is one of many that make slow cooking nearly foolproof, meaning it's fine to leave your food all day long without worrying that you'll come back to a burnt mess.

Slow cookers typically have multiple heat settings. "Low" and "high" settings (around 190°F and 300°F, respectively) are standard on most models, but some also have a "medium" setting. For this book, you'll need a slow cooker with at least low and high settings—pretty basic! More sophisticated slow cookers have temperature sensors that monitor the heat and adjust the heating element as necessary to keep the food cooking at an even temperature.

If you want to get really high-tech, some slow cookers offer sauté functions and computerized timing devices that can switch the heat levels automatically, turn off the cooking when the time is up, or keep the food warm after the cooking has completed. If your slow cooker has a sauté function, you can use it to brown the meat before proceeding with the slow cook setting. That way you dirty only one dish. But of course, the recipes in this book don't require this additional step. The goal here is simplicity and ease.

A Guide to Basic Slow Cooking

Although slow cooking is the ultimate hands-off activity, there are still some steps that you can take to ensure that meals go off without a hitch. In this section, I'll walk you through the important elements of prepping, cooking, and cleanup.

SAFETY AND SLOW COOKING

Before you dive into the slow cooker recipes in this book, you may understandably have some questions about the safety of your slow cooker. I did, too. (Although my concerns may have stemmed from the fact that I got my first slow cooker from the free bin of a garage sale.) As long as you follow a few basic guidelines, slow cooking—even over many hours—is a safe process.

Although a slow cooker typically keeps food at a lower temperature than a stovetop does, the low, direct heat is high enough to kill any harmful bacteria that could form during the cooking process. Slow cookers typically use very little electricity and can safely stay plugged in overnight or while you're away from home for hours.

Stay out of the danger zone. According to the US Department of Agriculture, bacteria grows most rapidly between 40°F and 140°F, doubling in number in as little as 20 minutes. Therefore, never leave uncooked food, especially meat or eggs, in the slow cooker for more than an hour before cooking begins. When the food is done cooking, either serve it within 1 hour or keep the slow cooker on warm (above 140°F) until you're ready to serve.

Thaw any frozen foods first. To ensure that the food reaches a safe temperature, never place frozen food into your slow cooker. Using frozen foods increases your chances of getting a foodborne illness, especially if you're cooking with meat. Any frozen ingredients should be thawed before cooking. (I make a handful of exceptions in this book only for foods that are unlikely to cause foodborne illness if they thaw slowly, such as fruits.)

Avoid raw kidney beans. Kidney beans contain a toxic chemical that requires higher temperatures to deactivate. You should completely avoid raw kidney beans in a slow cooker. Canned kidney beans are fine.

Test the temperature. If you want to test the temperature level of the cooker, fill the pot two-thirds full with water, turn it on low, and take the temperature of the water after 2 hours. If the temperature is less than 185°F, there's a good chance that the heating element is broken, and the pot should be replaced.

Prepping

Prepping is typically the most hands-on part of the slow cooking process, but it shouldn't take too long. Many slow cooker cookbooks require over 30 minutes of chopping, dicing, and browning meat before starting the slow cooker. That defeats the purpose altogether! Hence, all the recipes in this book have prep times under 15 minutes.

Chopping herbs and vegetables and seasoning meat are the essential prep steps for most recipes in this book. Some recipes might also call for steps like removing skin from pieces of chicken, trimming fat from red meat, or cutting bigger portions of meat into smaller pieces to ensure the meat stays tender throughout the cooking process.

Although you can brown meat on the stovetop or toast spices before adding them to the cooker for added flavor, you can still get great results without these steps, and the recipes in this book don't require them.

Some recipes call for frozen ingredients that need to be completely thawed before you add them to the crock. If you have to add these ingredients at the start of cooking, thaw them in the refrigerator the night before. If you have to add them at the end, you can thaw them as the rest of the food cooks, depending on the cook time.

Cooking

Most slow cooker recipes involve putting the main ingredients in the pot, closing the lid, and not doing much else for several hours. But before you head off to work, surf, hike, or whatever it is that you like to do while your slow cooker makes dinner, consider these small details to make your meals come out perfectly.

Don't add that just yet! For some recipes, there are a handful of ingredients that must be added at the end of the cooking time to ensure maximum flavor and ideal texture. These include pasta, seafood, dairy, and fresh herbs. Trust me here. If you put pasta into your slow cooker for eight hours, it won't come out al dente. It will be more like mush. Instead, follow the recipe and keep these ingredients on the side until the last minute.

Follow the Goldilocks principle. Don't overfill your slow cooker, but don't underfill it either. The distribution of food inside the crock affects the way it cooks. Unfilled space can lead to quicker cooking, while filling the crock more than three-quarters full slows down cooking and alters the texture of the food. Instead, aim for just right: a little less than three-quarters full.

Layer it on. As a rule of thumb, put the ingredients that take the longest to cook at the bottom of the crock. When you want meat to stew in liquid, stir it in among the other ingredients. When you want it to remain distinct, place it on top of the other ingredients.

Timing matters. When you're cooking in a slow cooker, timing is more flexible than it is when you're cooking on the stove or in the oven, but it's still essential. Some cookers have built-in timers that will stop the cooking process when the time is up or lower the temperature to a "keep warm" setting. If your slow cooker doesn't have this feature, set a timer to make sure you don't overcook your food. Just because the food is cooking slowly doesn't mean you won't end up with mush if you leave it in for too long.

Don't peek. Although the temptation to peek under the lid is real, trust that the cooker is doing its job. I know it's hard to wait, but lifting the lid early will release the heat and steam that's cooking and imparting flavor to the food, making it take even longer for the food to cook.

Finish it off with a flourish. The end of the cooking process for most recipes—the last 15 to 30 minutes—often involves a step or two where quick-cooking ingredients, like pasta or fresh herbs, are added. At this point, some recipes might also call for skimming fat from the dish, incorporating a thickener, removing bones from meat, stirring in cream or cheese, or blending or mashing some of the ingredients to change the texture of the dish. Don't skip these steps! They don't take long, and they really do make a difference.

Cleanup

Cleanup starts before you even start cooking with how you prep the interior of the crock. Some slow cookers work with disposable plastic liners, which you can find in most grocery stores. I prefer to coat the crock's interior with some oil before adding the ingredients to make cleanup easier. This adds a negligible amount of fat to the dish and no more plastic to the environment while preventing the food from sticking.

Most slow cookers have removable ceramic crocks and lids that can go into the dishwasher after cooking, but others should be washed by hand. Check your pot's user's manual for more details. Personally, I prefer to wash all of my cooking pots, pans, and knives by hand and place serving dishes and utensils in the dishwasher. I find that they last longer this way. But if you prefer the dishwasher, check the user's manual or flip the crock over and check the bottom for a label indicating whether the crock is dishwasher-safe. You should also wipe down the exterior of the slow cooker base with a soapy sponge or damp paper towel after using it.

To easily remove any stuck-on food bits inside the crock, fill the crock two-thirds full with water, and heat the liquid on low for a few hours. You can also add a bit of baking soda to the water to assist with the cleaning.

FOUR PERFECT SLOW COOKER OCCASIONS

The slow cooker excels at making meals on a daily basis, but did you know it also shines on special occasions? I love going all out for cocktail parties and holidays. But there's a limit to the number of bite-size appetizers and multicourse meals I can create. The slow cooker extends my capabilities, allowing me to make another dish or two with minimal effort.

HOLIDAYS Whatever holidays you celebrate, they're all about being with the people you love, not hovering over a hot stove (unless that's your thing!). The slow cooker makes it easy to cook your favorite holiday meals, such as mashed potatoes, holiday dressing, posole, or chicken soup with matzo balls.

CAR CAMPING The beauty of car camping is that you don't have to carry your food on your back. (I grew up backpacking, so this benefit is never lost on me.) The slow cooker lets you prepare a meal ahead of time, pack it in the car, and then use a car power inverter to prepare soups, stews, and other one-pot meals right at your campsite.

COCKTAIL PARTIES Here's where I'm guilty. When I throw a cocktail party, I want to make everything. The slow cooker lets me give in to my culinary ambitions without requiring hours of hands-on attention.

POTLUCKS The slow cooker solves a critical challenge with potlucks: keeping the food from getting cold. Not only does the slow cooker keep dishes warm in transport, it can also be plugged in to maintain the temperature. Food tastes better (and it's safer) when kept at 140°F or above.

Stocking the Slow Cooker Kitchen

Is there anything better than opening the refrigerator or looking in the pantry and discovering you have everything you need to make a tasty meal? That's what this section aims to prepare you for. To get the most out of your slow cooker, keep these ingredients on hand. They will come up in many recipes throughout this book, so they're worth the modest investment if you don't already have them.

Refrigerator Staples

Here are a handful of ingredients I try to always have on hand. They're great for cooking in general and especially for slow cooking.

Butter. Stir a few tablespoons of butter into soups and stews to enhance the flavor. Both salted and unsalted butter are acceptable.

Carrots. Along with celery and onions, carrots are part of a typical mirepoix, a common flavoring used as a base for soups and other recipes.

Celery. This is one of three ingredients in the French mirepoix, which is a foundation of flavor in many dishes.

Fresh herbs. I keep fresh parsley and cilantro in my refrigerator at all times because they add a fresh element to food, especially food prepared in the slow cooker. For maximum freshness, store fresh herbs in a jar with one to two inches of water, like you would with flowers in a vase. Tent the herbs with a plastic bag. Thyme, rosemary, and basil are nice to have on hand in the refrigerator or on a kitchen windowsill.

Heavy (whipping) cream. Because milk can be somewhat unstable in the slow cooker, I prefer to stir in heavy cream at the end of the cooking time. The fat keeps it stable and lends a luxurious creaminess to the dish. (Starch stabilizes dairy, so you will find a few recipes throughout that include dairy at the beginning of the cooking time.)

Lemons. A squeeze of fresh lemon juice brightens up nearly any dish. I keep a bowl of lemons in my refrigerator. They spoil too quickly when they're left out on the counter unless you use them in less than a week.

Pantry Staples

These pantry ingredients will be used over and over again in the recipes in this book.

Coconut milk. Whether you prefer a dairy-free diet or not, you can use coconut milk in many dishes. It has a subtle coconut flavor and creaminess. Unlike dairy, it can be used in the slow cooker at the beginning of the cooking process.

Cumin. This versatile spice has a pungent aroma and is used often in Latin American and Indian food. Use ground cumin or cumin seeds if you have a mortar and pestle for lightly grinding them.

Garlic and onions. I keep garlic and red and yellow onions on hand at all times. Store them in an uncovered container in a dark pantry away from potatoes, which will make them spoil faster.

Paprika. Paprika adds gorgeous red color and subtle spice to an array of dishes. I prefer smoked paprika because of the complexity and subtle smokiness it offers.

Pepper. I call for freshly ground black pepper throughout this book. It's far more flavorful than pre-ground pepper. Grinding the pepper yourself also keeps you from accidentally over-seasoning your dish. Either black peppercorns or rainbow peppercorns are acceptable.

Red pepper flakes. This seasoning is the easiest way to add some heat to your foods without chopping up a chile (and getting it on your hands). A little goes a long way, so start with a pinch and work up from there.

Salt. This might sound obvious, but good salt is an essential component of good food. Use kosher salt or fine sea salt for the best results. If you only have table salt, reduce the volume of salt called for in these recipes by half, then adjust the seasoning after cooking.

Soy sauce. Soy sauce adds both salt and umami flavors to many Asian dishes. Chefs debate exactly what the definition of umami is, but its literal Japanese translation is "deliciousness." It's also thought of as meaning savory.

Stewed tomatoes. Stewed tomatoes are an easy, essential component for soups, stews, and chilis. You can crush canned whole plum tomatoes with your hands for maximum flavor or use canned diced tomatoes for maximum convenience.

Stock or broth. Use low-sodium chicken or vegetable broth for recipes that call for broth. Technically, broth is made from meat and vegetables (or vegetables only), whereas stock is made from bones. But the two are used somewhat interchangeably outside of haute cuisine. Try the Low-Sodium Chicken Broth (page 124) or Vegetable Broth (page 125), both of which can be made in advance and then refrigerated or frozen, so you'll always have it ready to go. Quality store-bought versions are also fine.

Tomato paste. Even for dishes that don't sound tomatoey, a tablespoon or two of tomato paste adds savory, sweet, and acidic notes, which make just about anything taste better.

Four Steps to Maximize Flavor

If it doesn't taste good, what's the point? That's how I feel about food. Sure, food gives you energy and keeps you healthy, but at the end of the day, it has to taste good. Here are a few tips and tricks to help you maximize flavor in your slow cooker.

Aim for balance. The essence of good cooking is balanced flavors. This foundational concept has been taught in culinary schools and used by home cooks globally for centuries. More recently, it was made popular by the bestselling book *Salt, Fat, Acid, Heat: Mastering the Elements of Good Cooking* by Samin Nosrat. For this cookbook, I've built balance into every recipe. Once the food has finished cooking, taste it. Then consider adding a pinch of sea salt, swirling in a tablespoon of butter or olive oil, or adding a splash of red wine vinegar or lemon juice until it tastes so good you just can't help yourself from taking another bite.

Brown meat before cooking it. Although it takes a little extra time, browning meat before putting it in the slow cooker really amps up the flavor. Pat the meat dry with paper towels, then season it generously with salt and black pepper. Heat a skillet over high heat. When it's hot, lower the heat to medium-high. Pour in just enough oil to coat the pan. Sear the meat on all sides until it's well browned, about 3 to 5 minutes per side depending on the type of meat.

Use fresh herbs. Sturdy herbs like fresh thyme, rosemary, oregano, and sage can be added to the slow cooker at the beginning of the cooking time. Save delicate herbs such as cilantro, tarragon, and basil for sprinkling on the dish after it's cooked. Parsley is versatile and can go either way.

Use fresh spices. Use fresh spices (less than two years old), and consider toasting them in a dry skillet before adding them to the slow cooker. Toasting the spices isn't essential, but it can really maximize their flavor.

Cooker Companions

To get the most out of a slow cooker, there are a few things you should have handy in your kitchen. I'm not talking about spiralizers or blowtorches here, just everyday tools you'll use all the time. Although you can spend some cash on gadgets that make prepping, serving, and cleanup even faster or easier, you certainly don't have to. You will get a lot of mileage out of the affordable essentials listed here.

Equipment Essentials

Blender. A countertop blender is useful for pureeing soups. Always make sure to vent the lid when blending hot foods. An immersion or "stick" blender is also handy. With this tool, you can blend the soup right in the slow cooker.

Chef's knife. This tool does 90 percent of the work in my kitchen. I use it for chopping vegetables, nuts, herbs, meat, seafood, you name it! Get a good-quality knife, keep it sharp, and store it away from all other utensils, which might blunt it.

Cutting board. A wooden or bamboo cutting board is my first choice. Plastic is a fine second choice, but know that it doesn't provide any increased protection from foodborne illnesses. It harbors more meat bacteria than bamboo does. Never, ever use a glass cutting board unless you hate your knives and want to lose a finger. Glass is pretty, but it's not a good cutting surface.

Digital meat thermometer. Most of the time you won't need this because meat cooks for several hours in a slow cooker. But if you're like me and want to ensure that it has reached the correct internal temperature, buy a digital meat thermometer. Here are the minimum safe internal temperatures for the most common meats: pork, 145°F; beef, 125°F (rare); chicken, 165°F; fish, 145°F.

Grater. A fine grater is useful for zesting citrus and grating hard cheeses, garlic, and ginger. A box grater will work for cheeses, but it doesn't produce equally fine shreds.

Spatulas and wooden spoons. To avoid scratching the interior of your slow cooker crock, use a wooden spoon. Silicone spatulas are also helpful for removing all of the food from the slow cooker.

FROM THE SEA TO THE SLOW COOKER

The slow cooker is not the ideal tool for cooking seafood if you're looking for a set-it-and-forget-it recipe that can cook for hours. However, some types of fish can cook for about 1 hour or be added near the end of the cooking time.

Have you ever heard of dishwasher salmon? You wrap the fish in parchment paper, place it on the top rack of the dishwasher, and run the dishwasher. The same concept works for the slow cooker. You can wrap sturdy fish, such as salmon or mahi mahi, in parchment paper and slow cook it on low for about 1 hour.

Braised and poached fish can also be prepared in the slow cooker. Slow cook the other ingredients for the specified length of time, then add the fish and simmer for about 20 minutes, or until barely cooked through. Try the Fish Veracruz (page 88) or Cioppino (page 89), both of which use this cooking method.

Another seafood that can work well in a slow cooker is shellfish, such as mussels, clams, and shrimp. All you need to do is add the shellfish during the last few minutes of cooking, return the lid to the slow cooker, and simmer until all of the mussels and clams have opened (discard any that don't open after 10 minutes) and the shrimp are opaque (before they curl up tightly). If you want a dish with shrimp, try the Shrimp Boil (page 86).

The one fish I would never cook in a slow cooker is tuna. Tuna is best when quickly seared on each side and left rare in the middle, a job the slow cooker is not well suited for.

Nice-to-Have Gear

Here are a few pieces of gear that are nice to have but not essential.

Fat skimmer. As its name suggests, a fat skimmer removes fat floating at the top of the food while leaving any broth behind.

Insulated carriers. The slow cooker crock already retains heat during transport, but it's a little unwieldy. Use an insulated carrier to keep even more of that heat locked in and easily carry your slow cooker wherever it needs to go.

Lid latches. Lid latches keep the lid on tightly, which hastens cooking time slightly and is important if you're transporting your slow cooker anywhere. Many slow cookers come with silicone lid latches. But you can also buy them separately.

Metal claws for meat. Stainless steel meat forks make quick work of shredding, pulling, lifting, and serving meat.

Silicone roast racks. These sit at the bottom of your slow cooker and promote even heating. They also prevent meats from burning and sticking, and they help release and drain grease and fats into the pan.

Troubleshooting

Even when you follow a recipe perfectly, sometimes things don't come out according to plan. Here are a few issues that new slow cooker users run into, along with solutions to these problems.

What do I do when meat comes out dry or tough? For beef, pork, and lamb, add another 2 cups of liquid, such as water or broth, and cook for another 2 hours on low, which will help tenderize the meat. For chicken, unfortunately, the damage is done. Consider shortening the cooking time the next go around and using bone-in pieces of meat, which stay moist and tender for longer.

How do I fix food when it is too watery? For foods that are separated such as beef and broth, use a soup ladle to carefully remove liquid from the top. Remove as many spoonfuls as needed to produce the desired consistency. For foods that are more integrated, such as a pureed soup, make a slurry of 2 tablespoons of flour and 2 tablespoons of the cooking liquid. Mix this together in a separate container, then add it to the slow cooker. Simmer for another 30 minutes, or until the dish is thickened to your liking.

How do I fix food that is cooking unevenly? If your dish is cooking unevenly, remove the portion that's done, if possible, to a separate container. Then continue cooking what is left in the slow cooker until it reaches your desired level of doneness. One way to proactively address this is to cut foods that cook slowly into smaller pieces.

FIVE DISHES TO GET STARTED

I put together a list of recipes here that, apart from tasting delicious, are intended to help you learn how to use your slow cooker.

Banana-Nut Oatmeal (page 18). Wake up to the comforting aroma of banana bread in the form of oatmeal. This basic slow cooker recipe is an everyday staple that can be adapted to include whatever fruit and nuts you have on hand. With just 5 minutes of prep the night before, you can have breakfast ready when you wake up.

Sweet-and-Sour Meatballs (page 37). This mid-century staple has become an iconic, and in some circles an ironic, addition to the cocktail party menu. Tender meatballs simmer in a sauce of pineapple juice, tomato, and loads of brown sugar. It's virtually foolproof.

Chicken Fajita Chili (page 52). If you want a meal with minimal prep and maximum flavor, make this chicken fajita chili. Bottled enchilada sauce does all the heavy lifting, ensuring a delicious meal with minimal fuss.

Classic Baked Beans (page 56). If cooking beans from scratch intimidates you, use the slow cooker. Cooking low and slow will make the beans tender and delicious.

Carnitas Street Tacos (page 107). In these street tacos, shredded pork fills small corn tortillas that fit in the palm of your hand. They're topped with onion, jalapeño, cilantro, and lime juice. They're impressive and easy, a win-win.

What if my food takes too long to cook? If it's 6 p.m. and you're ready for dinner but your slow cooker meal is still an hour or more away from being finished, you can turn up the heat to high, switch to a pressure cooker setting (if you're using a multi-cooker), or transfer the food to a stovetop. For future dishes, plan on an increased cooking time and/or increase the heat to high for at least some portion of the cooking time. Also, make sure your slow cooker is still functioning properly.

Can I still cook with my slow cooker if my crock or lid cracks? If the slow cooker crock or lid cracks, refrain from cooking in it and request a replacement from the manufacturer. It could crack further and allow liquid to escape, which would damage the heating element and be unsafe.

The Recipes in this Book

The recipes in this book are written for a 6-quart oval cooker, the most common variety of slow cooker. Most dishes yield 6 to 8 servings and have cooking times of 8 hours or longer, so they can cook while you are out of the house.

The recipes are a mix of American dishes and international favorites, all of which can be prepared with simple ingredients found at most grocery stores. Each recipe includes dietary labels at the top indicating whether it is dairy-free, gluten-free, nut-free, vegan, or vegetarian, as well as tips at the bottom including serving suggestions, variations, prep ideas, and storage information.

Unlike some slow cooker books that require you to cook a portion of the meal separately on the stovetop, all of the cooking in these recipes happens inside the slow cooker. There are no steps requiring microwave or stovetop cooking. That said, some of the tips include optional variations you can try using the stove.

I hope that these recipes lead to years of happy slow cooking.

French Toast with Berries, page 21

Breakfast

Banana-Nut Oatmeal

Prep time: **5 minutes** / Cook time: **8 hours on low** / Serves: **6 to 8**
Vegetarian

With just five minutes of prep the night before, you can wake up to the comforting aromas and flavors of banana bread in the form of oatmeal. This breakfast is hearty enough to keep you satisfied until lunchtime and easy enough to clean up with minimal fuss.

1 tablespoon butter, plus more for serving

2 cups oats

2 bananas, mashed

½ cup finely chopped walnuts

1 teaspoon ground cinnamon

¼ teaspoon sea salt

6 cups water

1 cup whole milk or dairy-free milk, for serving

Brown sugar, for serving

1. Coat the interior of the slow cooker crock with the butter, making sure to cover about two-thirds up the sides of the crock.

2. Put the oats, bananas, walnuts, cinnamon, salt, and water in the crock. Stir gently to mix.

3. Cover and cook on low for 8 hours. Serve with the milk, additional butter, and brown sugar.

VARIATION TIP: This basic slow cooker recipe can be adapted to whatever fruit and nuts you have on hand. Try raisins, sliced apples, peaches, dried cranberries, or dried blueberries. For nuts, I love slivered almonds and crushed pecans.

Apple-Cinnamon Steel-Cut Oats

Prep time: **10 minutes** / Cook time: **8 hours on low** / Serves: **6 to 8**
Nut-Free / Vegetarian

This recipe practically screams fall. It's loaded with sweet apples, spicy cinnamon, and plump raisins. Steel-cut oats have a decidedly different texture than old-fashioned rolled oats or instant oatmeal. They are more akin to polenta or porridge. Steel-cut oats also tend to retain their distinct texture in the slow cooker more than other types do.

1 tablespoon butter, plus more for serving

2 cups steel-cut oats

2 apples, peeled, cored, and diced

1 cup raisins

1 cup apple juice

2 teaspoons ground cinnamon

¼ teaspoon sea salt

2 tablespoons brown sugar, plus more for serving

3 cups water

1. Coat the interior of the slow cooker crock with the butter, making sure to cover about two-thirds up the sides of the crock.

2. Put the oats, apples, raisins, apple juice, cinnamon, salt, brown sugar, and water in the crock. Stir gently to mix.

3. Cover and cook on low for 8 hours. Serve hot with additional butter and brown sugar.

NUTRITION TIP: Technically, you can purchase gluten-free oats and steel-cut oats from grocery stores, health food stores, or online. However, many people with celiac disease and non-celiac gluten intolerance still can't stomach oats due to their similar protein structure. If you can enjoy gluten-free oats, feel free to use them. No changes to the recipes are needed.

Salted Caramel and Peach Steel-Cut Oats

Prep time: **10 minutes** / Cook time: **8 hours on low** / Serves: **6 to 8**
Nut-Free / Vegetarian

Cream, brown sugar, and vanilla coalesce into a sweet syrup drenching this everyday breakfast staple in sweet decadence. As indulgent as it sounds, this breakfast only has a tablespoon of sugar and half a tablespoon of heavy cream per serving. If peaches are in season, use fresh ones to really bring this recipe to life. Their season is short though, so use thawed frozen peaches or canned peaches in a pinch. Just don't settle for mealy, unripe peaches from the produce section in January. They bring nothing to the party.

1 tablespoon butter, plus
   more for serving
2 cups steel-cut oats
2 peaches, peeled, pitted,
   and sliced
½ cup heavy
   (whipping) cream
½ cup brown sugar
1 tablespoon vanilla extract
1 teaspoon sea salt
4 cups water

1. Coat the interior of the slow cooker crock with the butter, making sure to cover about two-thirds up the sides of the crock.

2. Put the oats, peaches, cream, brown sugar, vanilla, salt, and water in the crock. Stir gently to mix.

3. Cover and cook on low for 8 hours. Serve with additional butter.

SERVING TIP: If you're really feeling fancy, sprinkle flaky sea salt over the oatmeal when you serve it. It adds texture and amps up the flavor of every bite.

French Toast with Berries

Prep time: **10 minutes** / Cook time: **2 hours on high** / Serves: **6 to 8**
Nut-Free / Vegetarian

Have you ever tried to make French toast for a crowd? It's a lot of standing around, flipping, and waiting for breakfast. No one eats at the same time. This slow cooker version yields eight servings with no fuss and no waiting—at least not active waiting. It takes two hours on high heat, so prepare it the night before, start it in the morning when you wake up, and you'll have an amazing brunch ready to eat.

1 tablespoon butter, plus more for serving
2 cups whole milk
6 large eggs
1 tablespoon vanilla extract
½ teaspoon ground cinnamon
1 loaf artisan white bread (see tip), cut into 2-inch pieces
2 (6-ounce) containers mixed berries, such as blueberries, raspberries, and strawberries
Maple syrup, for serving

1. Coat the interior of the slow cooker crock with the butter, making sure to cover about two-thirds up the sides of the crock.

2. In a bowl, whisk together the milk, eggs, vanilla, and cinnamon.

3. Put the bread and berries in the slow cooker and pour the egg mixture over the top. Gently tap the slow cooker crock on the countertop to ensure the egg mixture settles into any air pockets.

4. Cover and cook on high for 2 hours. Serve with additional butter and the maple syrup.

INGREDIENT TIP: Good-quality French bread, challah, and Texas toast all work well in this recipe. Although you can use everyday white bread, the texture won't be quite the same.

Peachy Cream Cheese Casserole

Prep time: **10 minutes** / Cook time: **6 to 8 hours on low** / Serves: **6 to 8**
Nut-Free / Vegetarian

Somewhere between a cheesecake, bread pudding, and a quiche, this sweet breakfast casserole is for those mornings when you want to celebrate. For me, that's after a long surf at dawn with my mates. In this recipe, ignore anything I told you about cooking with dairy in your slow cooker. The starch in the bread stabilizes the milk. Using full-fat dairy also helps.

1 tablespoon butter

6 cups cubed white bread

4 cups peeled, pitted, and sliced peaches

8 ounces cream cheese, cut into 1-inch pieces

12 eggs

1 cup half-and-half

¼ cup brown sugar

1 teaspoon vanilla extract

½ teaspoon sea salt

1. Coat the interior of the slow cooker crock with the butter, making sure to cover about two-thirds up the sides of the crock.

2. In the crock, layer half of the bread, half of the peaches, and half of the cream cheese in that order. Repeat with the remaining bread, peaches, and cream cheese. It doesn't have to be perfect; the goal is to distribute each of the ingredients throughout without stirring.

3. In a bowl, whisk together the eggs, half-and-half, brown sugar, vanilla, and salt. Pour the mixture into the crock.

4. Cover and cook on low for 6 to 8 hours, or until the casserole is fully set. Let it cool for at least 10 minutes before serving.

VARIATION TIP: Replace the peaches with 2 pints of fresh raspberries and ½ cup of sliced almonds.

Cheesy Slow Cooker Grits

Prep time: **10 minutes** / Cook time: **8 hours on low** / Serves: **6 to 8**
Gluten-Free / Nut-Free / Vegetarian

These easy slow cooker grits are the perfect backdrop for a fried egg and a few slices of bacon. Like many of the other recipes in this book that call for dairy, this one recommends you stir in the dairy just before serving.

4 tablespoons
  butter, divided
2 cups stone-ground
  yellow grits
1½ teaspoons sea salt
8 cups water
1 cup heavy
  (whipping) cream
2 cups shredded sharp
  cheddar cheese

1. Coat the interior of the slow cooker crock with 1 tablespoon of butter, making sure to cover about two-thirds up the sides of the crock.

2. Put the grits, salt, and water in the crock. Stir gently to mix.

3. Cover and cook on low for 8 hours.

4. Stir in the cream, cheese, and the remaining 3 tablespoons of butter. Serve hot.

INGREDIENT TIP: It's best to avoid instant grits in this recipe. White grits will work in a pinch, but the yellow, stone-ground variety will have a better texture and flavor. Note that some brands market stone-ground yellow grits as polenta, so go ahead and use that if that's what they have at the store.

Cranberry and Sweet Potato Quinoa

Prep time: **10 minutes** / Cook time: **6 to 8 hours on low** / Serves: **6 to 8**
Dairy-Free / Gluten-Free / Vegan

Quinoa is naturally rich in protein, more so than other grains. Technically, quinoa isn't a grain at all, making it a perfect gluten-free breakfast cereal. You can take quinoa in a sweet or savory direction. I prefer sweetness in the morning, so I loaded up on cinnamon, maple syrup, and dried cranberries for this recipe. But if you prefer savory, try the Southwestern Sweet Potato Quinoa (page 25).

1 tablespoon canola oil, or nonstick cooking spray

2 cups quinoa, rinsed

2 cups almond milk or other plant-based milk

2 medium sweet potatoes, peeled and diced

½ cup dried cranberries

1 teaspoon ground cinnamon

¼ teaspoon ground nutmeg

½ teaspoon sea salt

3 cups water

¼ cup maple syrup

1. Coat the interior of the slow cooker crock with the oil or spray it with nonstick cooking spray.

2. Put the quinoa, almond milk, sweet potatoes, cranberries, cinnamon, nutmeg, salt, and water in the crock. Stir gently to mix.

3. Cover and cook on low for 6 to 8 hours, until the quinoa is tender.

4. Stir in the maple syrup and serve, or drizzle the syrup over individual portions.

COOKING TIP: This dish may be ready in 6 hours, especially if your slow cooker tends to cook a little bit faster. If you're making it overnight, set your slow cooker timer to stop after 6 hours and keep the dish warm. If you don't have a timer, 8 hours is acceptable; the texture will be just a bit softer.

Southwestern Sweet Potato Quinoa

Prep time: **10 minutes** / Cook time: **6 to 8 hours on low** / Serves: **6 to 8**
Dairy-Free / Gluten-Free / Nut-Free / Vegan

Smoked paprika and ground cumin liven up this savory quinoa dish. It's loaded with protein and is equally at home on the dinner table. Alternatively, top this dish with a fried egg for a breakfast that will help you power through until lunchtime.

1 tablespoon canola oil, or nonstick cooking spray

2 cups quinoa, rinsed

4 cups Vegetable Broth (page 125), or store-bought

2 medium sweet potatoes, peeled and diced

1 cup canned black beans, drained and rinsed

1 cup frozen corn kernels, thawed

1 teaspoon ground cumin

1 teaspoon smoked paprika

1 teaspoon sea salt

¼ cup minced fresh cilantro

1 lime, halved

1. Coat the interior of the slow cooker crock with the oil or spray it with nonstick cooking spray.

2. Put the quinoa, vegetable broth, sweet potatoes, black beans, corn, cumin, paprika, and sea salt in the crock. Stir gently to mix.

3. Cover and cook on low for 6 to 8 hours, or until the quinoa is tender.

4. Stir in the cilantro and squeeze the lime halves over the top. Serve.

INGREDIENT TIP: If you're not a fan of cilantro—and some people genetically aren't—swap it out with flat-leaf parsley or sliced scallions.

Sausage and Potato Casserole

Prep time: **10 minutes** / Cook time: **6 to 8 hours on low** / Serves: **6 to 8**
Gluten-Free / Nut-Free

This recipe reminds me of the sausage egg muffins I grew up eating, when fast food was a real treat. There was something about the eggs, cheese, and sausage nestled between two pieces of toasted English muffin that really hit the spot. If you're feeding a crowd, or even just a few, this casserole makes quick work of the fast-food classic (okay, it takes all night, but you'll be sleeping). Serve with toasted English muffins if you like.

1 tablespoon butter

6 cups frozen hash browns, thawed

1 pound cooked, crumbled breakfast sausage

12 eggs

1 cup half-and-half

3 cups shredded cheddar cheese

1 teaspoon sea salt

1. Coat the interior of the slow cooker crock with the butter, making sure to cover about two-thirds up the sides of the crock.

2. In the crock, layer half of the hash browns and half of the sausage. Repeat with the remaining hash browns and sausage. It doesn't have to be perfect; the goal is to distribute the ingredients throughout without stirring.

3. In a bowl, whisk together the eggs, half-and-half, cheese, and salt. Pour the mixture into the slow cooker.

4. Cover and cook on low for 6 to 8 hours, or until the casserole is fully set. Let it cool for at least 10 minutes before serving.

VARIATION TIP: You can also use diced ham or cooked, crumbled bacon in place of the sausage. To make it vegetarian, opt for plant-based sausages.

Spicy Broccoli and Cheese Breakfast Casserole

Prep time: **10 minutes** / Cook time: **6 to 8 hours on low** / Serves: **6 to 8**
Gluten-Free / Vegetarian

I rarely sneak veggies into breakfast, but this one-dish, vegetarian, crustless quiche is tasty enough that even my kids don't mind something green on their plates. The bell pepper adds some color and sweetness. The recipe calls for pepper jack cheese, but if you prefer to use a blend of cheddar and jack, that's fine, too.

1 tablespoon butter
6 cups frozen hash
  browns, thawed
4 cups diced broccoli
1 red bell pepper, diced
12 eggs
1 cup half-and-half
2 cups shredded pepper
  jack cheese
1½ teaspoons sea salt

1. Coat the interior of the slow cooker crock with the butter, making sure to cover about two-thirds up the sides of the crock.

2. In the crock, layer half of the hash browns, half of the broccoli, and half of the bell pepper. Repeat with the remaining hash browns, broccoli, and bell pepper. It doesn't have to be perfect; the goal is to distribute each of the ingredients throughout without stirring.

3. In a bowl, whisk together the eggs, half-and-half, cheese, and salt. Pour the mixture into the crock.

4. Cover and cook on low for 6 to 8 hours, or until the casserole is fully set. Let it cool for at least 10 minutes before serving.

INGREDIENT TIP: If you prefer to use fresh potatoes, scrub 6 medium russet potatoes under running water and pat them dry. Peel the potatoes and grate them using a box grater or, better yet, a food processor. Taking one handful of potatoes at a time, squeeze out as much liquid as you can, then add them to the recipe.

Spinach-Artichoke Dip, page 33

CHAPTER 3

Snacks and Appetizers

Applesauce

Prep time: **15 minutes** / Cook time: **8 hours on low or 4 hours on high** / Serves: **6 to 8**
Dairy-Free / Gluten-Free / Nut-Free / Vegan

There is no better vessel for making applesauce than the slow cooker. Not only does this appliance cook the apples down beautifully into a luxurious sauce, it does so with minimal attention on your part. The best apples for homemade applesauce are Fuji, Gala, Honeycrisp, and Golden Delicious. I also like to toss a few Granny Smith apples in for their tartness. But really, whatever's available in your region or on sale at the grocery store will work just fine.

3 pounds apples, peeled, cored, and diced

1 teaspoon ground cinnamon

1 teaspoon lemon juice

Pinch sea salt

1. Combine the apples, cinnamon, lemon juice, and salt in the slow cooker crock.

2. Cover and cook on low for 8 hours or on high for 4 hours, stirring once or twice during the cooking process to keep the apples from sticking to the crock.

3. Use an immersion blender to puree the apples until smooth. You can also carefully transfer the mixture to a countertop blender and puree until smooth.

VARIATION TIP: Transform applesauce into apple butter! After blending the applesauce, stir in ⅔ cup of brown sugar and return the applesauce to the slow cooker. Leave uncovered and cook on high for 1 hour, stirring frequently. The mixture will reduce by nearly half and develop a deep golden-brown hue. Delicious!

Candied Pecans

Prep time: **10 minutes** / Cook time: **3 hours on low** / Serves: **6 to 8**
Gluten-Free / Vegetarian

These candied pecans make the perfect party snack. They also make a beautiful gift. Store leftovers (what's that?) in a covered container at room temperature. Any kind of hot sauce will do for this recipe, but my favorite is Cholula bottled hot sauce, which can be found in most grocery stores.

8 tablespoons (1 stick) butter, melted

¼ cup brown sugar

1 teaspoon hot sauce

1 teaspoon sea salt

1 pound whole untoasted pecans

1. In a large bowl, mix together the butter, brown sugar, hot sauce, and salt. Stir in the pecans and toss until well coated.

2. Transfer the pecan mixture to the slow cooker crock.

3. Cover and cook on low for 3 hours, stirring every 30 minutes to keep the pecans from burning.

4. Spread out the mixture onto a large baking sheet and let it cool to room temperature.

5. Store the pecans in a covered container at room temperature for up to 1 week.

SERVING TIP: If by some chance you don't eat all of the pecans the moment they're cool enough to handle, they're amazing on a mixed green salad with pomegranate arils, crumbled blue cheese, and sliced red onions, tossed with a homemade balsamic vinaigrette.

Rice Cereal Party Mix

Prep time: **10 minutes** / Cook time: **3 hours on low** / Serves: **12**
Gluten-Free / Vegetarian

You can buy premade party mixes at the grocery store, but once you make this mix at home, you'll never go back. This version is hot, fresh, and loaded with tasty spices. Another cool thing about making a party mix yourself is that you can adjust the cereal and nuts you use. I cannot eat wheat, so I make it with rice cereal and gluten-free pretzels. Also, if you're sensitive to peanuts, you can use toasted cashews instead.

8 cups rice cereal, gluten-free if desired

2 cups pretzels or pretzel sticks, gluten-free if desired

1 cup roasted unsalted peanuts

6 tablespoons (¾ stick) butter, melted

3 tablespoons Worcestershire sauce

2 teaspoons sea salt

Pinch cayenne pepper

½ teaspoon garlic powder

½ teaspoon onion powder

1. Combine the cereal, pretzels, and peanuts in the slow cooker crock.

2. In a bowl, whisk together the butter, Worcestershire sauce, salt, cayenne, garlic powder, and onion powder. Pour the butter mixture over the cereal mixture and stir well to mix.

3. Cover and cook on low for 3 hours, stirring about every 45 minutes to make sure it doesn't burn.

4. Spread the mixture out onto a large baking sheet and let it cool to room temperature.

5. Store in a covered container at room temperature for up to 1 week.

INGREDIENT TIP: If you're vegan or avoiding gluten, check the label on the Worcestershire sauce as it many contain anchovies and/or wheat. If you prefer, you can use 2 tablespoons of tamari or gluten-free soy sauce instead.

Spinach-Artichoke Dip

Prep time: **10 minutes** / Cook time: **2 to 3 hours on low** / Serves: **6 to 8**
Gluten-Free / Nut-Free / Vegetarian

Just in case you thought spinach and artichokes sounded healthy, let me assure you, there's nothing innocent about this rich, creamy dip. The two veggies play backup to a star-studded cast of dairies: cream cheese, sour cream, mozzarella, and Parmesan cheese. Unlike other recipes in this book where I advise leaving dairy out until the end, the length of cooking time and the nature of the other ingredients make it work in this recipe.

1 tablespoon butter

1 (8-ounce) bag frozen spinach, thawed

1 (12-ounce) jar quartered artichoke hearts, drained

½ tablespoon minced garlic

4 scallions, thinly sliced

8 ounces cream cheese, cut into 1-inch pieces

1 cup sour cream

1 cup shredded mozzarella cheese

1 cup grated Parmesan cheese (not the canned stuff)

Freshly ground black pepper

Cut up assorted vegetables, for serving

Sliced baguette, for serving

1. Coat the interior of the slow cooker crock with the butter, making sure to cover about two-thirds up the sides of the crock.

2. Squeeze as much of the excess liquid from the spinach as you can. You should be left with a relatively small handful. Put it in the crock along with the artichoke hearts, garlic, scallions, cream cheese, sour cream, mozzarella, and Parmesan. Stir gently to mix.

3. Cover and cook on low for 2 to 3 hours, or until the cheese is melted. Stir, taste, and add black pepper as desired. Serve with the vegetables and sliced baguette.

INGREDIENT TIP: If you prefer to use fresh spinach, blanch it first in boiling water for about 30 seconds. Rinse it under cool running water and squeeze out all the excess liquid. Then follow the recipe as instructed.

Chicken Enchilada Dip

Prep time: 5 minutes / Cook time: **2 hours on low** / Serves: **6 to 8**
Gluten-Free / Nut-Free

Just about anything tastes better when it's eaten with a tortilla chip as a utensil, especially chicken enchiladas. In this creamy, smoky, spicy dip, chipotle powder permeates the enchilada sauce, while cream cheese and shredded cheddar balance the acidity.

1 tablespoon butter

1 pound chicken tenderloins

1 (15-ounce) can red
  enchilada sauce

½ tablespoon minced garlic

½ teaspoon chipotle powder

8 ounces cream cheese, cut
  into 1-inch pieces

1 cup shredded
  cheddar cheese

Freshly ground black pepper

4 scallions, thinly sliced

Tortilla chips, for serving

1. Coat the interior of the slow cooker crock with the butter, making sure to cover about two-thirds up the sides of the crock.

2. Put the chicken, enchilada sauce, garlic, and chipotle powder in the crock. Stir until mixed.

3. Cover and cook on low for 2 hours. Using two forks or meat claws, shred the chicken.

4. Add the cream cheese and cheddar to the crock. Stir until well blended. Taste, and add black pepper as desired.

5. Sprinkle with the scallions and serve with tortilla chips.

SERVING TIP: To make individual portions of this dip, divide it between several ramekins. Top with an additional tablespoon of shredded cheddar cheese, then place the ramekins under a broiler for about 90 seconds, just until the cheese is bubbling.

Buffalo Wings

Prep time: **10 minutes** / Cook time: **3 hours on low** / Serves: **6 to 8**
Gluten-Free / Nut-Free

I'm on a three-ingredient recipe kick in my home right now. Sure, most of the time I'm using ingredients that are already prepared—like pasta, sauce, and sausages—but that doesn't really matter. When you're in a hurry, buy the best prepared brands you can and go for it! No one said you had to do it all yourself, and it doesn't get any easier than these buffalo wings. Just pick a buffalo sauce you adore, and you're good to go.

2 pounds chicken wings

1 (16-ounce) jar buffalo hot sauce

4 tablespoons (½ stick) butter, melted

1. Combine the chicken wings, buffalo sauce, and melted butter in the slow cooker crock.

2. Cover and cook on low for 3 hours, until the wings are cooked through. Serve hot.

COOKING TIP: Although not essential, broiling the slow-cooked wings gives them a sticky, crispy finish. Broil them on high for 3 to 4 minutes, flip, and broil for another 3 minutes.

Chicken Lettuce Wraps

Prep time: **10 minutes** / Cook time: **2 to 3 hours on high** / Serves: **8**
Dairy-Free / Gluten-Free / Nut-Free

This appetizer has all the appearance of a fancy party dish with brilliant colors, contrasting textures, and a pretty presentation, but the slow cooker does most of the work for you. The fish sauce is optional, but it is an authentic Southeast Asian ingredient and adds a nice "what is that?" element to the dish.

FOR THE CHICKEN

2 pounds boneless skinless chicken thighs, roughly chopped

1 tablespoon minced ginger

1 tablespoon minced garlic

Pinch red pepper flakes

1 tablespoon fish sauce (optional)

2 tablespoons soy sauce, gluten-free if desired

1 tablespoon toasted sesame oil

Sea salt

Freshly ground black pepper

FOR THE LETTUCE WRAPS

1 head butter lettuce

Handful fresh cilantro, roughly chopped

1 carrot, grated

2 limes, cut into wedges

TO MAKE THE CHICKEN

1. Put the chicken, ginger, garlic, red pepper flakes, fish sauce (if using), soy sauce, and sesame oil into the slow cooker crock. Season with salt and black pepper.

2. Cover and cook on high for 2 to 3 hours, until the chicken is cooked through.

TO ASSEMBLE THE LETTUCE WRAPS

3. To serve, place a spoonful of the chicken mixture in the center of a lettuce leaf. Top with a pinch of cilantro and grated carrot and finish with a squeeze of lime juice.

INGREDIENT TIP: A little goes a long way with toasted sesame oil. I find it useful in all kinds of dishes, but if you prefer not to use it, swap it with canola oil or another neutral vegetable oil.

Sweet-and-Sour Meatballs

Prep time: **10 minutes** / Cook time: **3 hours on low** / Serves: **6 to 8**
Dairy-Free / Nut-Free

My mother-in-law shared this recipe with me, and the first time I saw it, I was shocked. Grape jelly? Who knew? Apparently, that's the not-so-secret ingredient in tasty sweet-and-sour meatballs. I added diced pineapple, another classic ingredient in this dish, which I think adds to its deliciousness.

1 (12-ounce) bottle chili sauce

1 (12-ounce) jar grape jelly

1 (15-ounce) can pineapple chunks, undrained

2 pounds frozen meatballs, thawed

1. Combine the chili sauce, grape jelly, and the juice from the canned pineapple in the slow cooker crock. Whisk until well combined.

2. Add the pineapple chunks and meatballs. Stir very gently to coat the meatballs in the sauce.

3. Cover and cook on low for 3 hours, until the meatballs are cooked through. Serve hot.

COOKING TIP: To make it easier to whisk in the grape jelly, soften the jelly first by warming the jar (with the lid off) in the microwave for about 30 seconds.

Posole, page 44

CHAPTER 4

Soups, Stews, and Chilis

Potato Leek Soup

Prep time: **10 minutes** / Cook time: **6 to 8 hours on low** / Serves: **6 to 8**
Gluten-Free / Nut-Free

Leeks have a subtlety and sweetness that's not present in onions. I use them for both balance and complexity in this soup. Served with a loaf of crusty whole-grain bread, this dish makes a perfect light dinner, or you can serve it as a starter before a larger meal.

2 leeks, cleaned and
   thinly sliced
1 medium yellow onion,
   thinly sliced
4 medium russet potatoes,
   peeled and diced
2 garlic cloves, peeled
   and smashed
2 thyme sprigs, or
   ½ teaspoon dried thyme
8 cups Low-Sodium
   Chicken Broth (page 124),
   or store-bought
½ teaspoon sea salt, plus
   more if desired
½ cup heavy
   (whipping) cream
Freshly ground black pepper

1. Put the leeks, onion, potatoes, garlic, thyme, chicken broth, and salt into the slow cooker crock.

2. Cover and cook on low for 6 to 8 hours.

3. Remove the thyme sprigs, then stir in the cream.

4. Using an immersion blender, puree the soup until smooth or carefully transfer it to a countertop blender and puree until smooth. Taste, and season with additional sea salt and black pepper as desired.

INGREDIENT TIP: If you've never worked with leeks before, don't worry. They take just a couple of extra steps to prepare. Cut off about ⅔ of the dark green ends. Cut the leek lengthwise, nearly all the way through, revealing the many inner layers. Rinse the leeks under cold running water to remove all of the sediment that often gets trapped between the layers. Then cut them into slices.

Classic Minestrone

Prep time: **10 minutes** / Cook time: **8 hours 20 minutes on low** / Serves: **6 to 8**
Dairy-Free / Nut-Free / Vegan

Embrace the flavors of the Mediterranean in this healthy classic. I use borderline excessive amounts of garlic, fresh herbs, and olive oil for loads of flavor, which I think you'll love as much as I do.

2 (15-ounce) cans kidney beans, drained and rinsed

1 (28-ounce) can diced tomatoes, drained

1 cup chopped green beans

1 medium yellow onion, diced

2 carrots, diced

2 stalks celery, diced

1 tablespoon minced garlic

¼ cup roughly chopped fresh parsley

¼ cup roughly chopped fresh thyme

¼ cup roughly chopped basil

1 teaspoon sea salt, plus more if desired

8 cups Vegetable Broth (page 125), or store-bought

¼ cup extra-virgin olive oil

8 ounces elbow macaroni

Freshly ground black pepper

1. Put the kidney beans, tomatoes, green beans, onion, carrots, celery, garlic, parsley, thyme, basil, salt, vegetable broth, and olive oil into the slow cooker crock.

2. Cover and cook on low for 8 hours.

3. Add the macaroni, cover, and cook for another 15 to 20 minutes, or until the noodles are al dente. Taste, and season with salt and black pepper as desired.

INGREDIENT TIP: Although you might be tempted to use dry kidney beans here, don't! The slow cooker does not neutralize the natural toxins present in raw kidney beans. Use canned kidney beans instead.

Chipotle and Black Bean Soup with Lime Crema

Prep time: **10 minutes** / Cook time: **6 to 8 hours on low** / Serves: **6 to 8**
Gluten-Free / Nut-Free / Vegetarian

Chipotle peppers in adobo sauce bring spice, acidity, and a smoky note to any dish. Here, they liven up everyday black beans, making this simple soup absolutely crave-worthy. If you can take the heat, add the full 3 teaspoons of adobo sauce. Top with a tangy lime crema to cool things off.

FOR THE SOUP

4 (15-ounce) cans black
  beans, drained
1 tablespoon smoked
  paprika
1 tablespoon ground cumin
1 teaspoon ground coriander
1 chipotle pepper in adobo
  sauce, minced, plus 1 to
  3 teaspoons adobo sauce,
  as desired
¼ cup tomato paste
1 medium yellow
  onion, diced
1 tablespoon minced garlic
1 teaspoon sea salt
6 cups Vegetable
  Broth (page 125),
  or store-bought

FOR THE LIME CREMA

Zest and juice of 1 lime
1 teaspoon minced garlic
1 cup sour cream

TO MAKE THE SOUP

1. Put the black beans, paprika, cumin, coriander, chipotle pepper and adobo sauce, tomato paste, onion, garlic, salt, and vegetable broth into the slow cooker crock. Stir to mix.

2. Cover and cook on low for 6 to 8 hours, until some of the beans are broken down but others retain their shape.

3. Use an immersion blender to make the soup creamier, but don't fully puree it. You still want some texture from the beans.

TO MAKE THE LIME CREMA

4. In a small bowl, whisk together the lime zest and juice, garlic, and sour cream. Drizzle the crema over individual portions of soup.

COOKING TIP: If you have a multi-cooker, you can pressure cook dry beans and then proceed with the recipe on the "slow cook" setting. Use 1½ cups of dry beans and 6 cups of water. Pressure cook the soup for 45 minutes.

Chicken Enchilada Soup

Prep time: **10 minutes** / Cook time: **6 to 8 hours on low** / Serves: **6 to 8**
Gluten-Free / Nut-Free

Prepared enchilada sauce does the heavy lifting in this punchy soup, taking the place of multiple spices and lots of tomatoes. If you prefer a spicy soup, use a hot enchilada sauce. If you're serving it to kids or don't want the soup to be too hot, use a mild enchilada sauce. Several ingredients—corn, tomatoes, cheese, cilantro, and avocado—get stirred in after cooking. This ensures that they retain their fresh texture and that the cheese doesn't react to the acid in the enchilada sauce during cooking.

1 onion, diced

6 garlic cloves, minced

1½ pounds boneless
  skinless chicken thighs

1 (15-ounce) can black
  beans, drained and rinsed

1 (28-ounce) can red
  enchilada sauce

8 cups Low-Sodium
  Chicken Broth (page 124),
  or store-bought

Sea salt

Freshly ground black pepper

2 cups frozen corn
  kernels, thawed

2 plum tomatoes, diced

16 ounces shredded sharp
  cheddar cheese

1 avocado, peeled, pitted,
  and diced

1 cup chopped fresh
  cilantro (optional)

2 cups crisp tortilla strips,
  for serving (check label
  for gluten-free)

1. Put the onion, garlic, chicken, black beans, enchilada sauce, and chicken broth into the slow cooker crock. Stir to mix.

2. Cover and cook on low for 6 to 8 hours, until the onions are tender and the chicken is cooked through.

3. Using two forks or meat claws, shred the chicken into bite-size pieces. You may wish to transfer it to a cutting board to do this. If you do, return the chicken to the slow cooker after shredding it. Taste, and season with salt and black pepper, if desired.

4. Stir in the corn, tomatoes, cheese, avocado, and cilantro (if using).

5. Divide the soup between serving bowls and top with crisp tortilla strips.

COOKING TIP: Whenever you're using a prepared ingredient that isn't labeled "low-sodium," taste the food after it's cooked, then add some salt if you want. Canned foods, like enchilada sauce and chicken broth, are often loaded with sodium, and if you add a predetermined amount of salt, you'll end up oversalting the dish.

Posole

Prep time: **10 minutes** / Cook time: **8 to 10 hours on low** / Serves: **6 to 8**
Dairy-Free / Gluten-Free / Nut-Free

This crowd-pleasing soup is one of my favorites to order in authentic Mexican restaurants. I first tried it at a restaurant devoted to the foods of Mexico City, and it was incredibly delicious. There are two things to remember when making posole: be patient and allow the meat to cook, which is easy when you're using a slow cooker, and make sure you use the freshest, most flavorful toppings.

2 pounds pork shoulder

1 tablespoon ground cumin

1 tablespoon smoked paprika

1 tablespoon minced garlic

½ red onion, diced

1 teaspoon sea salt

1 (28-ounce) can hominy, drained

1 (28-ounce) can diced plum tomatoes, undrained

8 cups Low-Sodium Chicken Broth (page 124), or store-bought

2 avocados, peeled, pitted, and diced, for serving

1 bunch radishes, thinly sliced, for serving

2 cups thinly sliced green cabbage, for serving

4 limes, cut into wedges, for serving

1. Put the pork shoulder, cumin, paprika, garlic, onion, salt, hominy, plum tomatoes, and chicken broth into the slow cooker crock. Stir to mix.

2. Cover and cook on low for 8 to 10 hours. To speed things up, cook the soup on high for 2 hours, then lower the heat to low for the remaining 6 to 8 hours. The meat is done when it can be easily shredded with a fork.

3. Transfer the meat to a cutting board and, using two forks or meat claws, shred the meat. Return it to the slow cooker crock.

4. Divide the soup between serving bowls and top with avocados, radishes, cabbage, and a squeeze of lime juice.

INGREDIENT TIP: You can find hominy and smoked paprika in the Latin foods aisle of most grocery stores.

Ham and Split Pea Soup

Prep time: **10 minutes** / Cook time: **8 hours on low** / Serves: **6 to 8**
Dairy-Free / Gluten-Free / Nut-Free

The ham bone infuses this otherwise vegetarian soup with smoky flavors, making even humble split peas taste like a luxury. If you can't a find ham bone, opt for 1 cup of diced ham (not lunchmeat), which you can find in the meat section at the grocery store. Serve this soup with French bread in the dead of winter for a meal that will warm you to your core.

1 ham bone
2 cups dried green split
  peas, rinsed
1 carrot, diced
1 small yellow onion, diced
1 stalk celery, diced
4 garlic cloves, peeled
  and smashed
8 cups Low-Sodium
  Chicken Broth (page 124),
  or store-bought
1 thyme sprig, or
  ¼ teaspoon dried thyme
1 teaspoon sea salt, plus
  more if desired
Freshly ground black pepper

1. Put the ham bone, split peas, carrot, onion, celery, garlic, chicken broth, thyme, and salt into the slow cooker crock.

2. Cover and cook on low for 8 hours. Taste, and season with salt and black pepper as desired.

VARIATION TIP: To make this soup vegetarian, skip the ham bone and use smoked sea salt instead of regular sea salt. Swap the chicken broth for homemade Vegetable Broth (page 125) or a store-bought version.

Corn, Sausage, and Potato Soup

Prep time: **10 minutes** / Cook time: **6 to 8 hours on low** / Serves: **6 to 8**
Gluten-Free / Nut-Free

This soup combines tender gold potatoes, smoky sausage, and corn into a spicy, creamy broth. It reminds me of corn chowder but has all of the heft I'm looking for as warm summer days fade into cold autumn evenings. As usual, wait to stir in the cream until after cooking.

1½ pounds Yukon Gold potatoes, scrubbed and cut into 1-inch pieces

1 medium onion, diced

2 celery stalks, diced

4 garlic cloves, minced

8 ounces andouille or other cured sausage

2 cups frozen corn kernels, thawed

1 tablespoon Old Bay seasoning

8 cups Low-Sodium Chicken Broth (page 124), or store-bought

½ cup heavy (whipping) cream

Sea salt

Freshly ground black pepper

1. Put the potatoes, onion, celery, garlic, sausage, corn, Old Bay seasoning, and chicken broth in the slow cooker crock. Stir to mix.

2. Cover and cook on low for 6 to 8 hours.

3. Stir in the cream. Taste, and season with salt and black pepper as desired.

INGREDIENT TIP: If you cannot find a suitable cured sausage, feel free to use an uncooked pork sausage. Give it a quick sauté, until just cooked through, before adding it to the slow cooker.

Ribollita (Italian Bean Stew)

Prep time: **10 minutes** / Cook time: **6 to 8 hours on low** / Serves: **6 to 8**
Dairy-Free / Nut-Free / Vegan

Extra-virgin olive oil and day-old bread thicken this flavorful stew of vegetables, herbs, and beans. Don't be fooled—it's vegan but by no means light. This stew will warm you to your core and fill you up nicely. The exact mixture of herbs is not specified; just use what you have. If you only have parsley, that's fine. Thyme, basil, and rosemary really liven things up, too.

¼ cup extra-virgin olive oil

1 medium onion, diced

2 carrots, diced

2 celery stalks, diced

6 garlic cloves, minced

¼ teaspoon red
pepper flakes

½ cup roughly chopped
mixed fresh herbs, such as
parsley, rosemary, basil,
or thyme

4 cups Vegetable
Broth (page 125),
or store-bought

1 (28-ounce) can plum
tomatoes, crushed with
your hands

2 (15-ounce) cans
cannellini beans or other
white beans, drained
and rinsed

1 bunch lacinato kale, ribs
removed, thinly sliced

2 cups white bread,
crust removed, cut into
½-inch pieces

1. Put the olive oil, onion, carrots, celery, garlic, red pepper flakes, mixed herbs, vegetable broth, tomatoes, beans, kale, and bread in the slow cooker. Stir to mix.

2. Cover and cook on low for 6 to 8 hours, until the stew is thick and the vegetables are tender.

SUBSTITUTION TIP: Gluten-free bread works well in this soup. To keep it vegan, make sure to read the label of gluten-free breads, which are often leavened with egg whites.

Curried Red Lentil Stew

Prep time: **10 minutes** / Cook time: **6 to 8 hours on low** / Serves: **6 to 8**
Dairy-Free / Gluten-Free / Nut-Free / Vegan

Yellow curry powder is a powerhouse ingredient in this otherwise simple vegan dinner. Technically, curry powder is a blend of spices, the most predominant being turmeric, which gives curry powder its distinct golden hue. The better the quality of the curry powder, the better the flavors.

2 medium yellow
  onions, diced

½ tablespoon minced garlic

1 tablespoon minced ginger

1 tablespoon yellow
  curry powder

2 cups red lentils

6 cups Vegetable
  Broth (page 125),
  or store-bought

1 (15-ounce) can
  coconut milk

1 teaspoon sea salt

1 to 2 teaspoons lime juice

1. Combine the onion, garlic, ginger, curry powder, lentils, vegetable broth, coconut milk, and salt in the slow cooker. Stir to mix.

2. Cover and cook on low for 6 to 8 hours. Stir in the lime juice and serve.

INGREDIENT TIP: Always buy full-fat coconut milk. The lite version is just a watered-down version of full-fat and why pay for water? If you're concerned about the fat or calories, make your own lite coconut milk. Combine ¾ cup of full-fat coconut milk and ¾ cup of water. To thicken it, dissolve 1½ teaspoons of cornstarch in 2 tablespoons of water, then stir the cornstarch slurry into the coconut milk mixture. It will thicken within about 2 minutes of cooking.

Beef and Barley Stew

Prep time: **10 minutes** / Cook time: **8 to 10 hours on low** / Serves: **6 to 8**
Dairy-Free / Nut-Free

This one-pot meal has it all—tenderly stewed beef, vegetables, and grains. Like many of the soups and stews in this chapter, it's especially lovely in the cold fall and winter months. Barley is a whole grain, unlike pearl barley, which has the outer husk and bran layers removed. It has a similar texture to brown rice and contains gluten, so if you're gluten-free, opt for brown rice instead.

2 pounds beef chuck, cut into 2-inch cubes

1 medium yellow onion, minced

1 cup diced carrots

1 teaspoon minced garlic

1 tablespoon minced fresh rosemary

½ cup dry red wine

8 cups low-sodium beef broth

2 tablespoons tomato paste

1½ cups barley

1 teaspoon sea salt

1 teaspoon freshly ground black pepper

1. Put the beef, onion, carrots, garlic, rosemary, red wine, beef broth, tomato paste, barley, salt, and black pepper into the slow cooker. Stir to mix.

2. Cover and cook on low for 8 to 10 hours. Taste, and adjust the seasoning, if desired.

INGREDIENT TIP: Pretty much any cut of beef will work in this recipe, but there's no reason to waste money on an expensive cut like filet mignon. If you like, use a larger cut of beef that's still on the bone. It will add body to the stew as it cooks. After the cooking time has elapsed, remove the meat from the slow cooker, cut it into bite-size pieces, then return to the slow cooker along with any accumulated juices.

Moroccan Lamb Stew

Prep time: **10 minutes** / Cook time: **8 to 10 hours on low** / Serves: **6 to 8**
Dairy-Free / Gluten-Free

Ginger, curry powder, and citrus match the strong flavor of lamb in this stew, balanced by sweet dried apricots, briny olives, and crunchy roasted almonds. When picking olives, your best bet is to pop by the olive bar of an artisan market and choose a fresh green pitted variety. Serve this stew with long-grain white rice.

2 pounds boneless lamb shoulder, cut into 2-inch cubes

1 medium onion, halved and thinly sliced

1 tablespoon minced ginger

1 tablespoon minced garlic

2 carrots, diced

2 celery stalks, diced

¼ cup white wine

8 cups Low-Sodium Chicken Broth (page 124), or store-bought

Zest of one lemon, cut into long strips

2 tablespoons yellow curry powder

1 tablespoon smoked paprika

1 cup pitted green olives, such as Castelvetrano

1 cup roasted almonds

1 cup dried apricots, sliced

1 teaspoon sea salt

1 teaspoon freshly ground black pepper

1. Put the lamb, onion, ginger, garlic, carrots, celery, white wine, chicken broth, lemon zest, curry powder, paprika, olives, almonds, apricots, salt, and black pepper in the slow cooker crock. Stir to mix.

2. Cover and cook on low for 8 to 10 hours, or until the lamb is tender and the stew is very fragrant. Taste, and adjust the seasoning, if desired.

INGREDIENT TIP: When cutting the zest from the lemon, avoid cutting away too much of the white pith underneath. It is bitter and will give the stew an unpleasant flavor.

Farmers' Market Chili

Prep time: **10 minutes** / Cook time: **8 hours on low** / Serves: **6 to 8**
Gluten-Free / Nut-Free / Vegetarian

I have been making some version of this chili for the last 15 years since my friend Lynn shared her recipe with me. The trick to making a vegetarian chili that stands up to meaty versions is to introduce umami flavors. Literally translated as "deliciousness," umami is a Japanese word that has come to mean a lot of different things to American cooks. Technically speaking, it refers to naturally occurring glutamic acid. Plant-based versions of that include celery, mushrooms, and tomatoes. Although those might not seem like heavy hitters in the flavor world, they work together to make this chili really tasty.

2 medium yellow
  onions, diced
4 celery stalks, diced
4 carrots, diced
2 cups minced mushrooms
1 green bell pepper,
  thinly sliced
1 red bell pepper,
  thinly sliced
1 tablespoon minced garlic
2 (15-ounce) cans
  fire-roasted tomatoes
2 (15-ounce) cans pinto
  beans, drained and rinsed
1 tablespoon smoked
  paprika
1 tablespoon ground cumin
1 teaspoon ground coriander
1 tablespoon ancho
  chili powder
Sea salt
Freshly ground black pepper
½ cup sour cream,
  for serving

1. Put the onions, celery, carrots, mushrooms, green bell pepper, red bell pepper, garlic, tomatoes, beans, paprika, cumin, coriander, and chili powder into the slow cooker crock. Season generously with salt and black pepper. Stir to mix.

2. Cover and cook on low for 8 hours, or until all of the vegetables are tender. Taste, and adjust the seasoning, if desired. Serve with sour cream.

COOKING TIP: This recipe requires quite a bit of chopping. If you have a food processor, it can easily do the job. Just make sure not to cut the vegetables too finely, or they'll yield a watery chili.

Chicken Fajita Chili

Prep time: **10 minutes** / Cook time: **8 hours on low** / Serves: **6 to 8**
Gluten-Free / Nut-Free

Enjoy all of the flavors of chicken fajitas wrapped into a hearty chili. The predominant spice comes from the ancho chili powder, a dried version of the poblano pepper. It is barely sweet and smoky, with a mild heat, and it echoes the fresh poblanos used in this recipe.

2 pounds boneless skinless chicken thighs

2 green bell peppers, thinly sliced

2 red bell peppers, thinly sliced

2 poblano peppers, thinly sliced

2 medium yellow onions, halved and thinly sliced

1 (15-ounce) can fire-roasted diced tomatoes

2 (15-ounce) cans kidney beans, drained and rinsed

1 tablespoon ancho chili powder

1 teaspoon ground cumin

1 teaspoon smoked paprika

2 corn tortillas, thinly sliced

8 cups Low-Sodium Chicken Broth (page 124), or store-bought

Sea salt

Freshly ground black pepper

1 cup sour cream, for serving

1. Put the chicken, green bell peppers, red bell peppers, poblano peppers, onions, tomatoes, beans, ancho chili powder, cumin, paprika, corn tortillas, and chicken broth in the slow cooker. Season generously with salt and black pepper. Stir to mix.

2. Cover and cook on low for 8 hours. Taste, and adjust the seasoning, if desired. Serve with sour cream.

VARIATION TIP: If you can't find ancho chili powder, choose another mild chili powder. Just don't swap it for chipotle or cayenne. Both of those are fiery hot, and a full tablespoon would overwhelm the dish.

Five-Alarm Beef Chili

Prep time: **10 minutes** / Cook time: **8 to 10 hours on low** / Serves: **6 to 8**
Dairy-Free / Gluten-Free / Nut-Free

Giddy-up! This fiery beef chili has it going on. Tender beef chuck simmers in a sauce of three different kinds of peppers, fire-roasted tomatoes, and spices. This dish bypasses beans entirely and delivers a flavor punch that will have you reaching for a glass of water and a generous hunk of cornbread. Don't say I didn't warn you!

1 medium yellow onion, diced

2 red bell peppers, diced

1 tablespoon minced garlic

2 chipotle peppers in adobo sauce, minced, plus 2 teaspoons adobo sauce

2 jalapeño peppers, minced

1 tablespoon ancho chili powder

1 tablespoon ground cumin

1 teaspoon sea salt

1 teaspoon freshly ground black pepper

2 (15-ounce) cans fire-roasted diced tomatoes, undrained

2 pounds beef chuck, cut into 2-inch pieces or slightly smaller

1. Put the onion, bell peppers, garlic, chipotle peppers and adobo sauce, jalapeño peppers, ancho chili powder, cumin, salt, black pepper, tomatoes, and beef in the slow cooker crock. Stir to mix.

2. Cover and cook on low for 8 to 10 hours, or until the beef is tender.

INGREDIENT TIP: If you prefer a single-alarm chili or something without any heat at all, reduce or omit the chipotle. You can replace it with 1 tablespoon of smoked paprika and 1 teaspoon of red wine vinegar. Replace the jalapeño peppers with ½ of a green bell pepper, diced.

Herbed Mushrooms, page 63

CHAPTER 5

Vegetables and Sides

Classic Baked Beans

Prep time: **10 minutes** / Cook time: **6 hours on low** / Serves: **6 to 8**
Dairy-Free / Gluten-Free / Nut-Free

This summer picnic staple is perfect for the slow cooker. It can simmer for hours without heating up your kitchen or keeping you away from the pool. If you like bacon in your beans—I have been sensitive to the vegetarians in the crowd and left it out here—make sure to cook it first. Because I forego that traditional ingredient, I use smoked paprika to bring that yummy smoky flavor.

4 (15-ounce) cans pinto
beans, drained and rinsed
1 (4-ounce) can
tomato paste
½ cup brown sugar
1 tablespoon smoked
paprika
2 cups Low-Sodium
Chicken Broth (page 124),
or store-bought
Sea salt
Freshly ground black pepper

1. Put the beans, tomato paste, brown sugar, paprika, and chicken broth in the slow cooker crock. Season generously with salt and black pepper. Stir well to mix.

2. Cover and cook on low for 6 hours. (The canned beans are already cooked, so there is not a particular doneness cue.)

INGREDIENT TIP: To make this recipe using dried beans, soak 1 pound of pinto beans overnight in plenty of fresh water. Drain the beans, then put them in the slow cooker crock with 8 cups of Low-Sodium Chicken Broth (page 124) and the remaining ingredients. Cook for 8 to 10 hours on low. You may have heard that you cannot cook dry beans with salt. I believed this for a long time, and I was surprised to discover I had been wrong. Cooking dry beans with salt improves their flavor and texture, so make sure to season them well. The real enemy of dry beans is acidic ingredients, such as tomatoes, vinegar, or lemon juice, which hinder them from cooking to a soft, tender consistency.

Green Bean Casserole

Prep time: **10 minutes** / Cook time: **3 hours 30 minutes on low** / Serves: **6 to 8**
Nut-Free

The slow cooker is the perfect kitchen extender for holidays like Thanksgiving when the stovetop and oven are already spoken for. This is the only recipe in the book that calls for canned soup. As much as I like to cook from scratch, there are some recipes that demand sticking to tradition, and for me, this is one of them. I want it to taste just like my mom and my grandma made it. Another bonus: canned soup is easy-peasy.

2 pounds fresh green beans, trimmed and cut into 2-inch pieces

2 (15-ounce) cans cream of mushroom soup

1 cup Low-Sodium Chicken Broth (page 124), or store-bought

Sea salt

Freshly ground black pepper

2 cups crispy fried onions

1. Combine the green beans, cream of mushroom soup, and chicken broth in the slow cooker crock. Stir to mix.

2. Cover and cook on low for 3 hours, or until the green beans are very tender. Taste, and season with salt and black pepper as desired.

3. Top with the crispy fried onions, cover, and cook for an additional 30 minutes.

VARIATION TIP: To make this dish with canned green beans, use 6 (15-ounce) cans, drained. Omit the chicken broth and reduce the first cooking time to 2 hours.

Braised Red Cabbage

Prep time: **10 minutes** / Cook time: **4 to 6 hours on low or 2 hours 30 minutes on high**
Serves: **6 to 8**
Dairy-Free / Gluten-Free / Nut-Free / Vegan

This recipe began as a summer side dish for the grill, but as cooler weather brought us indoors, I reimagined it for the slow cooker. To replace the yummy smokiness of the grill, I added a teaspoon of smoked paprika. Any other smoked seasoning, such as smoked salt, will work as well.

1 small head red cabbage

1 cup Vegetable Broth (page 125), or store-bought

¼ cup extra-virgin olive oil

2 tablespoons balsamic vinegar

2 teaspoons Dijon mustard

1 teaspoon smoked paprika

½ teaspoon sea salt

¼ teaspoon freshly ground black pepper

1. Cut the cabbage into 8 wedges, cutting away the core just enough to remove it while leaving the wedges as intact as possible. It's okay if some separate. Place in the slow cooker crock.

2. In a bowl, whisk together the vegetable broth, olive oil, vinegar, mustard, paprika, salt, and black pepper, then pour the mixture over the cabbage.

3. Cover and cook on low for 4 to 6 hours or on high for 2 hours and 30 minutes, or until the cabbage is tender.

VARIATION TIP: For a more traditional braised cabbage, replace the balsamic vinegar with apple cider vinegar, and replace the paprika with a pinch of ground cloves.

Brown Sugar and Sage Carrots

Prep time: **10 minutes** / Cook time: **2 hours on high or 4 to 6 hours on low**
Serves: **6 to 8**
Dairy-Free / Gluten-Free / Vegetarian

If you're feeling in a fall mood but want a little more adventure than the standby pumpkin spice latte, this recipe is for you. Tender carrots bathe in a glaze of brown sugar, orange juice, and fresh sage. It's perfect at the Thanksgiving table or alongside an oven-roasted chicken or pork tenderloin.

¼ cup brown sugar
½ cup orange juice
2 sage sprigs, minced
2 pounds carrots
Sea salt
8 tablespoons (1 stick)
  butter, cut into pieces

1. In the slow cooker crock, whisk together the brown sugar and orange juice. Add the sage and carrots. Toss gently to coat them in the orange juice mixture. Season the carrots generously with salt.

2. Cover and cook on high for 2 hours or on low for 4 to 6 hours, until the carrots are very tender. Add the butter during the last 10 minutes of cooking.

INGREDIENT TIP: If you're making this recipe in the spring, give just-picked carrots a shot. Scrub the carrots clean and trim away all but 1 inch of their tender stems. Use the greens to make pesto.

Cauliflower Mash

Prep time: **5 minutes** / Cook time: **1 hour on high or 2 to 3 hours on low** / Serves: **6 to 8**
Gluten-Free / Nut-Free

Sometimes I want the creamy texture of mashed potatoes without all of the starch. This lighter version hits all the right notes with minimal carbs. It's also easily made vegan. Simply replace the chicken broth with almond milk and the butter with vegan butter.

1 large head cauliflower, cut into 2-inch pieces

½ cup Low-Sodium Chicken Broth (page 124), or store-bought

1 garlic clove, peeled and smashed

8 tablespoons (1 stick) unsalted butter, cut into pieces

½ teaspoon sea salt

1. Put the cauliflower, chicken broth, garlic, butter, and salt in the slow cooker crock. Stir to mix.

2. Cover and cook on high for 1 hour or on low for 2 to 3 hours, until the cauliflower is tender.

3. Using an immersion stick blender or a potato masher, mash the cauliflower until it's mostly free of lumps. Taste, and adjust the seasoning, if desired.

INGREDIENT TIP: There's no need to discard the stem from the cauliflower. Simply trim the tough end and discard the leaves.

Southern Collards

Prep time: **10 minutes** / Cook time: **3 to 4 hours on low or 1 hour 30 minutes to 2 hours on high** / Serves: **6 to 8**
Dairy-Free / Gluten-Free / Nut-Free / Vegan

Collard greens are the unsung heroes of the superfood world. They pale in comparison to kale in terms of popularity, but they're just as nutritious! I try to keep things healthy with this vegan take on Southern collard greens.

3 bunches collard greens, tough stems removed

1 teaspoon minced garlic

1 cup Vegetable Broth (page 125), or store-bought

2 tablespoons canola oil

2 tablespoons apple cider vinegar

1 tablespoon smoked paprika

1 teaspoon sea salt

¼ teaspoon red pepper flakes

1. Roll each of the collard greens into a tight cylinder and cut them into thin shreds.

2. Put the collards into the slow cooker crock with the garlic, vegetable broth, oil, vinegar, paprika, salt, and red pepper flakes. Stir to mix.

3. Cover and cook on low for 3 to 4 hours or on high for 1 hour 30 minutes to 2 hours, or until the greens are tender.

VARIATION TIP: This recipe also works well with other dark leafy greens, such as kale or mustard greens.

Braised Leeks

Prep time: **10 minutes** / Cook time: **4 hours on low** / Serves: **6 to 8**
Dairy-Free / Gluten-Free / Nut-Free / Vegan

Do you tend to think of leeks in the same way you think of onions or garlic? They're usually used as an ingredient in a dish, not the star of the show. This dish will have you rethinking that. Leeks simmer in a simple mix of olive oil and white wine with a generous sprinkle of salt and black pepper. Try serving them with Classic Meatloaf (page 95) or roasted chicken and polenta.

4 to 6 leeks
¼ cup extra-virgin olive oil
½ cup dry white wine
Sea salt
Freshly ground black pepper

1. Cut the dark green ends from the leeks and save for another purpose. You should have about 6 to 8 inches remaining. Cut the leeks in half lengthwise and rinse them under cool running water, peeling aside the layers to wash away any trapped sediment.

2. Arrange the leeks in the slow cooker crock, then add the olive oil and white wine. Season generously with salt and black pepper.

3. Cover and cook on low for 4 hours, or until the leeks are very tender.

INGREDIENT TIP: Leeks are in season October through May, fitting the cozy, comforting nature of this dish.

Herbed Mushrooms

Prep time: **10 minutes** / Cook time: **1 hour 30 minutes on high** / Serves: **6 to 8**
Dairy-Free / Gluten-Free / Nut-Free / Vegan

Herbed mushrooms are one of those side dishes I rarely think to make, but when I do, I can't stop snacking on them. They're also amazing sliced and used over burgers or as a pizza topping. Additionally, they make a great vegan meat alternative in tacos or enchiladas.

¼ cup extra-virgin olive oil

2 pounds baby portabella mushrooms, washed and tough ends trimmed

8 ounces shiitake, morels, or wild mushrooms, trimmed

½ cup minced fresh parsley

1 tablespoon minced garlic

1 teaspoon sea salt

1 teaspoon freshly ground black pepper

3 tablespoons dry sherry or water

1. Put the olive oil, portabellas, shiitakes, parsley, garlic, salt, black pepper, and sherry in the slow cooker crock. Stir gently to mix.

2. Cover and cook on high for 1 hour and 30 minutes, or until the mushrooms are soft and beginning to brown.

INGREDIENT TIP: A common mushroom myth is that you shouldn't wash them because they'll absorb water. That's not true! Chef Alton Brown did a fantastic video on this on his show *Good Eats*. It's totally worth the watch, and it illustrated that mushrooms don't take in water. But they do lose some dirt with a quick bath in cool water. So, if you're not keen on dirt, give them a rinse.

Cheesy Polenta

Prep time: **10 minutes** / Cook time: **2 hours on low** / Serves: **6 to 8**
Gluten-Free / Nut-Free / Vegetarian

Polenta is an underappreciated starch. There is a misconception that it's very labor intensive and requires a long time of hovering over a splattering pot on the stovetop. The reality is polenta actually does quite well when left mostly on its own. This version is so rich and creamy you might even want to swap your standby mashed potatoes for it.

2 cups hot water, divided
1 cup polenta
2 cups half-and-half
4 tablespoons
 (½ stick) butter
Sea salt
Freshly ground black pepper
1 cup grated Parmesan

1. In the slow cooker crock, whisk together 1 cup of hot water and the polenta until it is smooth with no lumps.

2. Add the remaining 1 cup of hot water, the half-and-half, and butter to the crock. Stir gently to mix. Season generously with salt and black pepper.

3. Cover and cook on low for 2 hours, stirring once or twice. Stir in the Parmesan. Taste, and adjust the seasoning, if desired.

INGREDIENT TIP: Look for coarse polenta, sometimes called corn grits or coarse cornmeal. Don't use regular fine cornmeal.

Gouda and Garlic Potatoes

Prep time: **10 minutes** / Cook time: **4 hours on high** / Serves: **6 to 8**
Gluten-Free / Nut-Free / Vegetarian

A generous dose of fresh garlic and fragrant thyme permeates this remixed version of scalloped potatoes. Gouda cheese melts well and brings a creamy texture and barely sweet flavor to the potatoes. You can use Gruyère instead of Gouda if you prefer.

1 tablespoon butter

2 cups heavy (whipping) cream

1 tablespoon minced garlic

1 tablespoon minced fresh thyme

½ teaspoon sea salt

½ teaspoon freshly ground black pepper

2 pounds russet potatoes, peeled and thinly sliced

1 cup shredded Gouda cheese

1. Coat the interior of the slow cooker crock with the butter, making sure to cover about two-thirds up the sides of the crock.

2. In a bowl, whisk together the cream, garlic, thyme, salt, and black pepper.

3. Spread a layer of potatoes in the bottom of the crock. Pour ¼ to ⅓ cup of the cream mixture over the top, then sprinkle 2 tablespoons of cheese over the potatoes. Repeat with the remaining potatoes, cream mixture, and cheese.

4. Cover and cook on high for 4 hours, or until the potatoes are tender.

INGREDIENT TIP: Although it's common for recipes for white or light-colored foods to call for white pepper, this one doesn't. Here's why: I don't like how white pepper smells or tastes. I would prefer a few black flecks in my creamy white potatoes if they'll taste better. Plus, most people have black pepper in their kitchen already.

Mashed Potatoes

Prep time: **10 minutes** / Cook time: **6 hours on low** / Serves: **6 to 8**
Gluten-Free / Nut-Free / Vegetarian

Raise your hand if you usually use boxed mashed potato flakes because making them from scratch seems like too much of an ordeal. I'm with you. The slow cooker actually works remarkably well for cooking potatoes until they're tender and easily mashed with a potato masher. The trick is to fold in the butter without too much stirring, which will make the mashed potatoes gummy. Whatever you do, please don't pull out the electric mixer—that will overmix the potatoes.

3 pounds russet potatoes, peeled and cut into 2-inch pieces

1 teaspoon sea salt

2 cups water

8 tablespoons (1 stick) butter, softened

1 cup sour cream

1. Put the potatoes, sea salt, and water into the slow cooker crock.

2. Cover and cook on low for 6 hours, until the potatoes are very tender.

3. Mash the potatoes with a potato masher until no lumps remain. Fold in the butter and sour cream, mixing just until combined. Taste, and adjust the seasoning, if desired.

VARIATION TIP: Need to omit the dairy? Use vegan butter and vegan sour cream.

Chickpea and Potato Puree

Prep time: **10 minutes** / Cook time: **6 hours on low or 2 hours on high** / Serves: **6 to 8**
Dairy-Free / Gluten-Free / Nut-Free / Vegan

One evening while visiting friends out of town, our hostess brought out this savory snack. Initially, I thought it was hummus. It's actually a slightly elevated version that functions equally well as a dip or as a backdrop for sautéed vegetables.

2 (15-ounce) cans
  chickpeas, drained
  and rinsed
1 medium russet potato,
  peeled and diced
2 sage leaves
1 rosemary sprig
½ cup extra-virgin olive oil
1 teaspoon sea salt
½ cup water

1. Combine the chickpeas, potato, sage, rosemary, olive oil, salt, and water in the slow cooker crock. Stir to mix.

2. Cover and cook on low for 6 hours or on high for 2 hours.

3. Remove the rosemary and sage. Using an immersion blender, puree until smooth, adding more water if needed to achieve a looser consistency.

SERVING TIP: Serve with rice crackers and top with sautéed greens, such as spinach or dandelion greens.

Ratatouille

Prep time: **15 minutes** / Cook time: **6 to 8 hours on low** / Serves: **6 to 8**
Dairy-Free / Gluten-Free / Nut-Free / Vegan

Like many Americans, I didn't know what ratatouille was until I watched the movie. Since then, I've been fascinated with the iconic dish. I've tried it with thinly sliced zucchini and eggplant, as it's done in the movie. I've salted the eggplant ahead of time to draw out moisture. And I've made it by cooking one vegetable at a time. (What a pain!) Tossing everything into the slow cooker is by far the easiest method and produces the same flavorful results you'd get from fussier preparations.

1 (28-ounce) can plum tomatoes, crushed with your hands

½ cup extra-virgin olive oil

1 large eggplant, cut into 1-inch pieces

2 medium zucchini, cut into 1-inch pieces

1 tablespoon minced garlic

1 teaspoon minced fresh thyme

¼ cup minced fresh parsley

Sea salt

Freshly ground black pepper

1 tablespoon balsamic vinegar

¼ cup roughly chopped fresh basil

1. Combine the tomatoes, olive oil, eggplant, zucchini, garlic, thyme, and parsley in the slow cooker crock. Season generously with salt and black pepper. Stir gently to mix.

2. Cover and cook on low for 6 to 8 hours, until the vegetables are tender.

3. Stir in the balsamic vinegar and basil. Taste, and adjust the seasoning, if desired.

INGREDIENT TIP: The somewhat generous portion of olive oil in this dish might seem like a lot, and it is. But it really makes the vegetables especially tender and sweet. Feel free to cut the amount in half if you must.

Root Vegetable Cassoulet

Prep time: **15 minutes** / Cook time: **6 to 8 hours on low** / Serves: **6 to 8**
Dairy-Free / Gluten-Free

Traditional French cassoulet can hardly be called a vegetable-centric dish. This reimagined version moves meat from the star of the show to a supporting role. (If you want a traditional meaty version, turn to page 78.) Instead, this cassoulet highlights tasty root vegetables and white beans cooked with andouille sausage. It tastes better the second day, so make it a day ahead if you can.

¼ cup extra-virgin olive oil

1 pound parsnips, peeled and diced

1 pound sweet potatoes, peeled and diced

2 turnips, peeled and diced

1 (15-ounce) can navy beans, drained and rinsed

8 ounces cured andouille sausage, cut into 1-inch pieces

1 medium yellow onion, diced

¼ cup minced celery

1 tablespoon minced garlic

1 teaspoon minced fresh sage

1 cup Low-Sodium Chicken Broth (page 124), or store-bought

Sea salt

Freshly ground black pepper

1. Combine the olive oil, parsnips, sweet potatoes, turnips, navy beans, sausage, onion, celery, garlic, sage, and chicken broth in the slow cooker crock. Stir gently to mix.

2. Cover and cook on low for 6 to 8 hours, until the vegetables are tender. Season generously with salt and black pepper.

VARIATION TIP: Use goose fat or duck fat in place of the olive oil to bring extra flavor to the dish and give it a touch of authenticity. You can find these ingredients in jars at mainstream grocery stores.

Cioppino, page 89

CHAPTER 6

Poultry and Fish

Honey-Teriyaki Chicken

Prep time: **10 minutes** / Cook time: **6 to 8 hours on low** / Serves: **6 to 8**
Dairy-Free / Nut-Free

Some nights, I need a recipe with as few ingredients as possible just to get dinner on the table. That said, I never want to sacrifice flavor. To me, dinner is always an event to be celebrated, and this recipe delivers both simplicity and flavor. Choose a good-quality bottled teriyaki sauce without high-fructose corn syrup. The garlic and red pepper flakes amp up the flavor, and the honey brings additional sweetness.

1 (16-ounce) bottle
   teriyaki sauce
¼ cup honey
4 garlic cloves, minced
Pinch red pepper flakes
2½ pounds bone-in
   skinless chicken thighs
Steamed white rice,
   for serving
4 scallions, thinly sliced,
   for serving
2 tablespoons sesame
   seeds, for serving

1. In the slow cooker crock, whisk together the teriyaki sauce, honey, garlic, and red pepper flakes. Add the chicken and turn the pieces to coat them in the sauce.

2. Cover and cook on low for 6 to 8 hours, until the chicken is tender. Spoon over steamed rice and garnish with the scallions and sesame seeds.

VARIATION TIP: Use microwavable instant rice to make this dish come together in a flash.

Orange Chicken

Prep time: **10 minutes** / Cook time: **6 to 8 hours on low** / Serves: **6 to 8**
Dairy-Free / Gluten-Free / Nut-Free

Traditional orange chicken has a crispy layer of batter and is deep-fried. As tasty as that is, sometimes I'm not too keen on heating up a vat of oil in my kitchen and getting my hands all sticky. (Plus, deep-frying brings back memories of when I was a young newlywed and set my kitchen on fire!) This slow cooker recipe has all the flavors of orange chicken without the risk or the mess.

1 cup orange juice

1 teaspoon orange zest

½ cup Low-Sodium
  Chicken Broth (page 124),
  or store-bought

¼ cup brown sugar

2 tablespoons rice vinegar

2 tablespoons gluten-free
  soy sauce

1 teaspoon minced ginger

1 teaspoon minced garlic

¼ teaspoon red
  pepper flakes

2 tablespoons cornstarch

2 tablespoons water

2 pounds boneless skinless
  chicken thighs

1. Combine the orange juice, orange zest, chicken broth, brown sugar, rice vinegar, soy sauce, ginger, garlic, and red pepper flakes in the slow cooker crock. Stir to mix.

2. In a bowl, whisk together the cornstarch and water until dissolved. Add the mixture to the slow cooker along with the chicken thighs and gently stir to mix.

3. Cover and cook on low for 6 to 8 hours, until the chicken is cooked through.

COOKING TIP: Whisking the cornstarch into the water before adding it to the slow cooker ensures you don't end up with any lumps in the sauce. This mixture is called a slurry. You can also mix flour and water or flour and broth to create a slurry to thicken soups and stews.

Coconut Milk–Braised Chicken

Prep time: **10 minutes** / Cook time: **6 hours on low** / Serves: **6 to 8**
Dairy-Free / Gluten-Free / Nut-Free

Creamy coconut milk and a generous hit of green curry paste infuse this chicken with flavors often found in Southeast Asian cooking. Braising is one of the most forgiving cooking techniques, and paired with the slow cooker, it's practically foolproof. Unlike poaching, which submerges food fully in liquid, braising uses a small amount of liquid, so the food cooks with indirect heat.

1 (14-ounce) can
  coconut milk
2 cups Low-Sodium
  Chicken Broth (page 124),
  or store-bought
¼ teaspoon red pepper
  flakes
½ medium yellow onion,
  halved and thinly sliced
¼ cup green curry paste
2 tablespoons brown sugar
1 pound green beans,
  trimmed and cut into
  2-inch pieces
2 pounds boneless skinless
  chicken thighs
Sea salt
Freshly ground
  black pepper
1 tablespoon lime juice
Gluten-free soy sauce,
  for serving

1. Combine the coconut milk, chicken broth, red pepper flakes, onion, curry paste, brown sugar, green beans, and chicken thighs in the slow cooker crock. Stir gently to mix. Season generously with salt and black pepper.

2. Cover and cook on low for 6 hours, until the chicken is cooked through and the vegetables are tender.

3. Stir in the lime juice. Serve with soy sauce.

INGREDIENT TIP: Green curry paste is a secret weapon of flavor. As much as I do enjoy hunting down galangal, lemongrass, and kaffir lime leaves then grinding them into a paste with a mortar and pestle, it's much easier to pop by the Asian section of the grocery store and snag a jar of curry paste. This recipe works equally well with red curry paste, too.

Chicken Adobo

Prep time: **10 minutes** / Cook time: **7 to 8 hours on low, plus 30 minutes on high**
Serves: **6 to 8**
Dairy-Free / Gluten-Free / Nut-Free

Pungent adobo chicken is a traditional Filipino dish made with soy sauce and vinegar. I have a major sour tooth, so I adore the bright, zingy flavors of this dish. At the end of the cooking time, I recommend simmering the sauce uncovered to allow it to reduce. (Some of the vinegar will evaporate during this step.) Consider opening a window for this because the aromas will be powerful!

½ cup white vinegar
½ cup gluten-free soy sauce
2 tablespoons brown sugar
1 teaspoon freshly ground
  black pepper
2 teaspoons minced garlic
2½ pounds bone-in
  skinless chicken thighs
2 tablespoons cornstarch
2 tablespoons water
Steamed jasmine rice,
  for serving

1. Combine the vinegar, soy sauce, brown sugar, black pepper, garlic, and chicken in the slow cooker crock. Gently stir to mix.

2. Cover and cook on low for 7 to 8 hours.

3. Increase the heat to high. Remove the lid, transfer the chicken to a serving dish, and cover it with aluminum foil. Continue simmering for another 30 minutes to reduce the sauce.

4. During the last 5 minutes of cooking, whisk together the cornstarch and water in a small bowl, and stir it into the sauce. Return the chicken to the slow cooker and coat the pieces in the sauce. Serve with the steamed jasmine rice.

INGREDIENT TIP: This recipe and others in this book call for bone-in chicken thighs. Other bone-in cuts of chicken, such as drumsticks, will work as well. Chicken breasts can easily dry out during long cooking times. However, using bone-in pieces will help keep them moist and tender.

Chicken Pot Pie

Prep time: **15 minutes** / Cook time: **6 hours on low, plus 2 hours on high** / Serves: **6 to 8**
Nut-Free

I love chicken pot pie. Who doesn't? But it's so much work spread out over so many steps. The slow cooker cuts down the process into two simple steps: cooking the filling and cooking the biscuits. It's the ultimate comfort food.

4 tablespoons butter, melted, divided

1 medium yellow onion, diced

2 carrots, diced

1 celery stalk, diced

1 pound Yukon Gold potatoes, peeled and diced

1 teaspoon minced garlic

1 teaspoon fresh thyme

¼ cup all-purpose flour

1 pound chicken thighs, cut into 1-inch pieces

4 cups Low-Sodium Chicken Broth (page 124), or store-bought

Sea salt

Freshly ground black pepper

2 cups frozen peas, thawed

1 (16-ounce) package refrigerated biscuits

1. Coat the interior of the slow cooker crock with 1 tablespoon of the melted butter, making sure to cover about two-thirds up the sides of the crock.

2. Put the onion, carrots, celery, potatoes, garlic, thyme, flour, chicken, chicken broth, and the remaining 3 tablespoons of melted butter in the crock. Season generously with salt and black pepper. Stir gently to mix.

3. Cover and cook on low for 6 hours.

4. Stir in the peas. Arrange the biscuits over the top of the chicken and vegetable mixture. Increase the heat to high, cover, and cook for 2 additional hours, or until the biscuits are puffy and golden.

VARIATION TIP: If you prefer a pie crust topping, use refrigerated pie crust and cut it to fit the shape of your slow cooker. Reduce the final cook time to 45 minutes on high.

Oktoberfest Chicken

Prep time: **10 minutes** / Cook time: **8 hours on low** / Serves: **6 to 8**
Dairy-Free / Nut-Free

My family immigrated to the United States from Germany during the mid-1800s, and my husband grew up in Germany during the 1980s. As a result, German food holds a special place in our hearts. This dish captures all of the classic flavors of Oktoberfest, and it's perfect during the fall and winter months.

1 tablespoon canola oil

1 medium onion, halved and thinly sliced

4 to 6 garlic cloves, peeled and smashed

3 apples, peeled, cored, and cut into 8 wedges

1 cinnamon stick

1 pound bratwurst sausages, cut into 1-inch pieces

2 pounds boneless skinless chicken thighs

16 ounces hard cider

Sea salt

Freshly ground black pepper

Stone-ground mustard, for serving

Kaiser rolls, for serving

1. Coat the interior of the slow cooker crock with the oil, making sure to cover about two-thirds up the sides of the crock.

2. Put the onion, garlic, apples, and cinnamon stick in the crock. Stir to mix. Top with the bratwurst and chicken and pour the hard cider over the top. Season generously with salt and black pepper.

3. Cover and cook on low for 8 hours, or until the meat is cooked through. Serve with the mustard and kaiser rolls.

VARIATION TIP: Transform this into a stew by cutting the chicken into 2-inch pieces and adding 8 cups of homemade Low-Sodium Chicken Broth (page 124) or a store-bought version.

Cassoulet

Prep time: **10 minutes** / Cook time: **8 hours on low** / Serves: **6 to 8**
Dairy-Free / Gluten-Free / Nut-Free

Low and slow. That's the traditional method for cooking cassoulet, and the slow cooker is the perfect vessel for convenient, all-day cooking. Cassoulet has its origins in southern France where it is typically made with duck or goose confit and sometimes mutton. (Try finding that in your local market!) Like many French recipes, it began as a peasant dish, a way to extend the life of the previous day's stew and use up bits and pieces of meat.

2 (15-ounce) cans navy
  beans, drained and rinsed
½ cup diced pancetta
8 ounces andouille sausage,
  cut into ½-inch slices
1 yellow onion, halved and
  thinly sliced
2 carrots, diced
8 garlic cloves, peeled
  and smashed
1 tablespoon herbs
  de Provence
½ cup dry white wine
2 cups Low-Sodium
  Chicken Broth (page 124),
  or store-bought
6 bone-in skinless
  chicken thighs
1 teaspoon sea salt
Freshly ground black pepper

1. Put the beans, pancetta, sausage, onion, carrots, garlic, herbs de Provence, wine, and chicken broth in the slow cooker crock. Stir gently to mix.

2. Season the chicken with the salt and black pepper and nestle the pieces in the bean mixture.

3. Cover and cook on low for 8 hours.

SUBSTITUTION TIP: For American cooks who may not have leftover andouille sausage lying around (I'm with you!) and can't find it at the local market, use another pork sausage, such as kielbasa, instead.

Chicken Tikka Masala

Prep time: **10 minutes** / Cook time: **6 to 8 hours on low** / Serves: **6 to 8**
Gluten-Free / Nut-Free

The ingredient list for this recipe is long, but if you have a well-stocked pantry, it should come together easily. Even if you don't have all these ingredients on hand, they are easily found in most grocery stores. Traditional spices include vibrant turmeric, pungent cumin, and coriander. In addition to making the dish taste amazing, they are also anti-inflammatory spices and useful in a wide variety of global cuisines. I make things easy by using a pinch of red pepper flakes instead of whole chiles. Serve with garlic naan or another flatbread and steamed rice.

2 pounds boneless skinless
  chicken thighs
1 medium yellow
  onion, diced
1 (15-ounce) can diced
  tomatoes
1 tablespoon ground
  turmeric
1 teaspoon ground coriander
2 teaspoons ground cumin
Pinch red pepper flakes
1 tablespoon minced garlic
1 tablespoon minced
  fresh ginger
2 cups Low-Sodium
  Chicken Broth (page 124),
  or store-bought
1 teaspoon sea salt
1 cup plain whole
  milk yogurt
½ cup heavy
  (whipping) cream
Chopped fresh cilantro,
  for serving

1. Combine the chicken, onion, tomatoes, turmeric, coriander, cumin, red pepper flakes, garlic, ginger, chicken broth, and salt in the slow cooker crock. Stir gently to mix.

2. Cover and cook on low for 6 to 8 hours. The chicken will be very tender, and the onion and tomatoes will be melded into a thick sauce.

3. Let rest uncovered for 10 minutes. Stir in the yogurt and cream. Serve with cilantro.

COOKING TIP: This is one of the recipes where you should not add the yogurt or cream at the beginning of the cooking time. The acids in the tomato will react to the milk solids and curdle it. Add the dairy products at the end as instructed, and the sauce will remain smooth and creamy.

Coq au Vin

Prep time: **10 minutes** / Cook time: **8 hours on low** / Serves: **6 to 8**
Gluten-Free / Nut-Free

Coq au vin sounds fancy—as does anything when you say it in French—but it's nothing more than chicken stewed in vegetables and wine and finished with butter. I prefer white wine to red in this recipe because it has a more delicate flavor, but either one will work fine. The trick to making the sauce absolutely luxurious is whisking in the cold butter. The milk solids react with the acid in the wine to produce a velvety, rich sauce.

1 medium yellow onion,
   halved and thinly sliced
8 ounces white button
   mushrooms, halved
6 garlic cloves, peeled
   and smashed
2½ pounds bone-in
   skinless chicken thighs
2 cups dry white wine
1 cup Low-Sodium Chicken
   Broth (page 124),
   or store-bought
2 thyme sprigs
Sea salt
Freshly ground black pepper
4 tablespoons (½ stick)
   cold butter, divided
¼ cup minced fresh parsley

1. Put the onion, mushrooms, garlic, chicken, wine, chicken broth, and thyme in the slow cooker crock. Season with salt and black pepper.

2. Cover and cook on low for 8 hours, until the chicken is cooked through.

3. Transfer the chicken and larger pieces of vegetables to a serving dish. Remove and discard the thyme sprigs.

4. Without turning off the slow cooker, whisk in the butter, 1 tablespoon at a time, until it's fully emulsified.

5. Carefully pour the sauce over the chicken. Top with the fresh parsley and serve with additional wine, if desired.

INGREDIENT TIP: Never use cooking wine. It usually has added salt and is poor quality. Instead, choose an inexpensive bottle that you wouldn't mind drinking. It's not the time to break out that fancy bottle you've been saving since your trip to Sonoma.

Cuban Chicken

Prep time: **10 minutes** / Cook time: **6 to 8 hours on low** / Serves: **6 to 8**
Dairy-Free / Gluten-Free / Nut-Free

Sweet, sour, and savory flavors permeate this hearty, one-pot chicken dinner as the sweetness of orange juice and raisins plays off the briny olives and grassy herbs. It is amazing served as a late summer dish when the weather's hot and you don't want to heat up your kitchen but you're eager for heartier fare. Serve with a glass of crisp, dry white wine.

½ cup minced fresh parsley
2 teaspoons dried oregano
Zest and juice of 1 lime
Zest and juice of 1 orange
½ cup pepper-stuffed olives
¼ cup raisins
2 green bell peppers, sliced
1 medium onion, halved and
  thinly sliced
8 garlic cloves, peeled
  and smashed
2 pounds bone-in skinless
  chicken thighs
1 pound Yukon Gold
  potatoes, cut into
  2-inch pieces
2 cups Low-Sodium
  Chicken Broth (page 124),
  or store-bought
Sea salt
Freshly ground black pepper
1 cup frozen peas, thawed

1. Combine the parsley, oregano, lime zest and juice, orange zest and juice, olives, raisins, bell peppers, onion, garlic, chicken, potatoes, and chicken broth in the slow cooker crock. Stir gently to mix. Season generously with salt and black pepper.

2. Cover and cook on low for 6 to 8 hours, until the chicken is cooked through and the potatoes are tender. Stir in the peas before serving.

INGREDIENT TIP: A whole chicken will work well in this recipe. Before placing it in the slow cooker, make sure to remove the skin and to season the chicken liberally with salt and black pepper to ensure that it's flavorful throughout. Extend the cook time to 8 to 9 hours.

Braised Chicken Breasts with Stewed Zucchini

Prep time: **10 minutes** / Cook time: **8 hours on low** / Serves: **6 to 8**
Dairy-Free / Gluten-Free / Nut-Free

The foundation for this one-pot chicken dinner is stewed zucchini, herbs, onions, and tomatoes. It has almost a ratatouille feel, without the eggplant. For me, zucchini is good two ways—either quickly sautéed so it's browned and caramelized on the edges or stewed until it's soft and melds well with other vegetables. This recipe delivers the latter option. It's the epitome of French comfort food.

2 zucchini

1 small red onion, diced

4 garlic cloves, peeled and smashed

¼ cup minced fresh parsley

1 tablespoon minced fresh rosemary

½ cup dry white wine

1 (28-ounce) can plum tomatoes

6 bone-in skinless chicken breasts

Sea salt

Freshly ground black pepper

1. Cut the zucchini in half lengthwise, then cut them into ½-inch pieces.

2. Combine the zucchini, onion, garlic, parsley, rosemary, wine, and tomatoes in the slow cooker crock. Stir gently to mix.

3. Place the chicken into the vegetable mixture and season generously with salt and black pepper.

4. Cover and cook on low for 8 hours, until the chicken is cooked through.

INGREDIENT TIP: Rosemary is an evergreen shrub that's easy to grow in many parts of the United States. It does well without too much care, and it's so nice to walk outside and snip a few sprigs. You can also grow it in a pot on a windowsill.

Jamaican Jerk Chicken

Prep time: **10 minutes** / Cook time: **6 to 8 hours on low** / Serves: **6 to 8**
Dairy-Free / Gluten-Free / Nut-Free

Traditional Jamaican jerk sauce combines Scotch bonnet peppers, onions, and garlic with a plethora of tasty spices, including allspice, cloves, and black pepper. You can make jerk sauce from scratch, or you can do what I do when I'm in a hurry—buy the bottled sauce. Using a bottled version means you won't need to gather 15 ingredients and prepare a sauce ahead of time. That's winning! Another bonus: you don't end up with nearly full bottles of allspice languishing in your spice drawer.

1 (12-ounce) bottle Jamaican jerk sauce

2 cups Low-Sodium Chicken Broth (page 124), or store-bought

2 pounds bone-in skinless chicken thighs

4 shallots, thinly sliced

2 garlic cloves, peeled and smashed

Zest and juice of 1 lime

4 cups steamed white rice, for serving

½ bunch fresh cilantro, roughly chopped

2 scallions, thinly sliced

1. Combine the jerk sauce, chicken broth, chicken, shallots, garlic, and lime zest in the slow cooker crock. Stir gently to mix.

2. Cover and cook on low for 6 to 8 hours, until the chicken is cooked through. Serve over white rice. Top with the cilantro, scallions, and drizzles of lime juice.

INGREDIENT TIP: Some recipes in this book call for shallots. If you're not familiar with them, please don't be intimidated. They're similar to red onions but have a more delicate flavor and texture. Shallots are available in nearly all grocery stores in the produce section near the onions and garlic.

Chicken Marsala

Prep time: **10 minutes** / Cook time: **6 to 8 hours on low, plus 17 minutes on high**
Serves: **6 to 8**
Nut-Free

Marsala is a fortified wine with an amber hue and nutty, dried fruit and honey flavors. It transforms everyday chicken and mushrooms into a meal to remember. Traditional chicken marsala is made with chicken that's coated in flour and seared. In this recipe, after the sauce reduces, it's further thickened with flour and butter.

½ cup marsala wine

1 cup Low-Sodium Chicken Broth (page 124), or store-bought

2 pounds boneless skinless chicken thighs

2 cups sliced mushrooms

1 small red onion or 4 shallots, minced

4 garlic cloves, minced

2 teaspoons fresh thyme

Sea salt

Freshly ground black pepper

2 tablespoons butter, melted

2 tablespoons all-purpose flour

1. Combine the wine, chicken broth, chicken, mushrooms, onion, garlic, and thyme in the slow cooker crock. Stir gently to mix. Season with salt and black pepper.

2. Cover and cook on low for 6 to 8 hours, until the chicken is cooked through.

3. Using a slotted spoon, transfer the chicken and mushrooms to a serving plate. Increase the heat to high and simmer, uncovered, for another 15 minutes, until the sauce is reduced by about a third.

4. In a small bowl, whisk the melted butter and flour together and then whisk it into the sauce in the slow cooker. Simmer until the sauce is thickened, about 2 minutes. Pour the sauce over the chicken and mushrooms and serve.

INGREDIENT TIP: Purchase a dry marsala wine from the wine section of the grocery store or at a liquor store. Don't be tempted by the marsala cooking wine in the vinegars and oils section of the market. It's usually loaded with salt and other additives.

Panang Duck Curry

Prep time: **10 minutes** / Cook time: **6 to 8 hours on low** / Serves: **6 to 8**
Dairy-Free / Gluten-Free / Nut-Free

Panang curry beautifully marries some unlikely partners: peanut butter, shrimp paste, tamarind, ginger, and garlic. This flavorful sauce is studded with sweet pineapple and savory bell peppers. If you're not feeling like duck, bone-in, skinless chicken legs will work fine in this recipe. They aren't quite as flavorful and fatty as duck, but they do the trick.

¼ cup panang curry paste

1 (14-ounce) can coconut milk

¼ cup brown sugar

Juice of 1 lime

2½ pounds bone-in skinless duck legs

8 ounces green beans, trimmed and cut into 2-inch pieces

1 (18-ounce) can pineapple chunks, drained

2 green bell peppers, sliced

1 cup roughly chopped fresh basil

1. Whisk together the curry paste, coconut milk, brown sugar, and lime juice in the slow cooker crock.

2. Add the duck, green beans, pineapple, and bell peppers to the crock.

3. Cover and cook on low for 6 to 8 hours. Stir in the basil after cooking.

VARIATION TIP: To make this recipe even easier, replace the curry paste, coconut milk, and brown sugar with 2 cups (16 ounces) of store-bought panang curry sauce.

Shrimp Boil

Prep time: **10 minutes** / Cook time: **4 hours on low, plus 15 to 20 minutes on high**
Serves: **6 to 8**
Dairy-Free / Gluten-Free / Nut-Free

Cooking with seafood in a slow cooker is tricky business. Most other ingredients can withstand hours, and in fact need hours, in the slow cooker. Not seafood! It cooks in as little as 15 minutes. Hence, most seafood recipes involve two phases. In this shrimp boil, potatoes and onions simmer in a spicy broth for four hours. Then shrimp, corn, and sausage join the party for the last 15 to 20 minutes of cook time. Why would you do this in a slow cooker instead of on the stovetop? Because it's mostly hands-off.

2 pounds Yukon Gold
  potatoes, cut into
  2-inch pieces

1 medium yellow onion, cut
  into eighths

4 garlic cloves, minced

¼ cup minced celery

2 bay leaves

8 cups Low-Sodium
  Chicken Broth (page 124),
  or store-bought

3 tablespoons Old
  Bay seasoning

3 corn ears, halved

1½ pounds jumbo shrimp,
  deveined and unpeeled

1 pound andouille sausage,
  cut into 1-inch pieces

Sea salt

Freshly ground black pepper

1. Put the potatoes, onion, garlic, celery, bay leaves, chicken broth, and Old Bay seasoning in the slow cooker crock. Stir gently to mix.

2. Cover and cook on low for 4 hours, or until the potatoes are tender.

3. Increase the heat to high. Add the corn, shrimp, and sausage.

4. Cover and cook for 15 to 20 minutes, until the shrimp is opaque and the sausage is warmed through. Season with salt and black pepper.

INGREDIENT TIP: Yukon Gold potatoes have a waxy texture that stays intact while they cook, as opposed to starchier potatoes that disintegrate into the broth.

Basque Fish

Prep time: **10 minutes** / Cook time: **6 hours on low, plus 20 to 30 minutes**
Serves: **6 to 8**
Dairy-Free / Gluten-Free / Nut-Free

Basque Country is an autonomous region of northern Spain with arguably some of the best cuisine in the world, if you're measuring by Michelin stars. One of the most iconic ingredients of the region is paprika. This one-dish meal features it prominently, alongside other regional staples like red peppers, artichokes, and potatoes.

1 (28-ounce) can plum tomatoes in basil, drained and crushed with your hands

1 (12-ounce) jar roasted red bell peppers, drained and sliced

1 (12-ounce) jar marinated artichoke hearts, drained

1 pound small Yukon Gold or fingerling potatoes, cut into 1-inch pieces, if needed

1 tablespoon paprika

¼ cup minced fresh parsley

¼ cup extra-virgin olive oil

2 pounds halibut

Sea salt

Freshly ground black pepper

1. Combine the tomatoes, roasted peppers, artichoke hearts, potatoes, paprika, parsley, and olive oil in the slow cooker crock. Stir gently to mix.

2. Cover and cook on low for 6 hours.

3. Add the halibut, cover, and cook for another 20 to 30 minutes, until the fish is cooked through. Season generously with salt and black pepper.

VARIATION TIP: Fish is a mainstay in coastal Basque Country, but this recipe is also tasty with chicken. If you prefer, add 2 pounds of bone-in chicken thighs in step 1. Cook on low for 8 hours.

Fish Veracruz

Prep time: **10 minutes** / Cook time: **6 to 8 hours on low, plus 20 minutes** / Serves: **6 to 8**
Dairy-Free / Gluten-Free / Nut-Free

This dish originated in the Mexican coastal town of Veracruz and consists of fish cooked in a salty, briny combo of onion, garlic, capers, tomatoes, and olives. For years, I purchased premade fish Veracruz from the frozen section of a grocery store—not exactly authentic. But it was convenient and tasty. This version successfully recreates the original from scratch in a slow cooker.

¼ cup extra-virgin olive oil
¼ cup dry white wine
1 medium yellow
 onion, minced
5 garlic gloves, minced
¼ cup capers, with about
 1 tablespoon of brine
1 pint grape tomatoes,
 halved
½ cup roughly chopped
 pitted green olives, such
 as Castelvetrano
1 to 2 jalapeño
 peppers, minced
1 tablespoon chopped
 fresh oregano
2 pounds red snapper,
 halibut, or tilapia
Sea salt
Freshly ground black pepper
¼ cup minced fresh parsley

1. Combine the olive oil, wine, onion, garlic, capers, tomatoes, olives, jalapeño pepper, and oregano in the slow cooker crock. Stir gently to mix.

2. Cover and cook on low for 6 to 8 hours, until the vegetables are tender.

3. Place the fish into the tomato mixture, and spoon the sauce over the fish. Season generously with salt and black pepper.

4. Cover and continue cooking for another 20 minutes, until the fish is barely cooked through and just begins to flake with a fork. Shower the fish with the fresh parsley before serving.

VARIATION TIP: The olive oil adds body and enhances the flavor of the dish. However, if you prefer a low-fat diet, you can omit it entirely. Add ¼ cup of water in its place to keep the ingredients from sticking to the slow cooker.

Cioppino

Prep time: **10 minutes** / Cook time: **6 to 8 hours on low, plus 10 to 15 minutes**
Serves: **6 to 8**
Dairy-Free / Gluten-Free

Cioppino originated in San Francisco in the early 1900s. Fishermen used the day's catch of fresh seafood to prepare a meal onboard their boats. This quickly spread to beachside seafood stalls and the city's restaurants, eventually becoming an iconic regional dish known as cioppino. In this slow-cooker version, onion, fennel, garlic, and tomatoes simmer away for hours to create a rich backdrop for whatever the day's catch is in your part of the world. The ingredient list is a little longer than most in this book, but this dish is worth it.

1 medium yellow
 onion, minced
1 fennel bulb, trimmed
 and diced
6 garlic cloves, peeled
 and smashed
8 cups low-sodium fish
 stock or Low-Sodium
 Chicken Broth (page 124)
1 (15-ounce) can crushed
 plum tomatoes
¼ cup extra-virgin olive oil
2 tablespoons tomato paste
½ cup dry white wine
Pinch red pepper flakes
1 pound mussels or
 littleneck clams
1 pound firm white fish,
 such as halibut, cut into
 1-inch pieces
8 ounces bay scallops
Juice of 1 lemon
½ cup chopped fresh
 parsley

1. Combine the onion, fennel, garlic, fish stock, tomatoes, olive oil, tomato paste, wine, and red pepper flakes in the slow cooker crock. Stir gently to mix.

2. Cover and cook on low for 6 to 8 hours, until the vegetables are tender.

3. Add the mussels and fish, cover, and cook until the mussels have opened, 10 to 15 minutes. Discard any mussels that haven't opened after 15 minutes.

4. Stir in the bay scallops and continue simmering for 2 to 3 minutes, or until the scallops are opaque. Stir in the lemon juice and parsley. Serve.

INGREDIENT TIP: This recipe works with many different types of seafood. If you have access to crab legs, shrimp, and other fresh fish, they'll all work well here. Add anything that's already cooked (such as crab legs) during the last few minutes of cooking.

Sunday Pot Roast, page 96

CHAPTER 7

Beef, Pork, and Lamb

Beer-Braised Beef Brisket

Prep time: **10 minutes** / Cook time: **8 to 10 hours on low** / Serves: **6 to 8**
Dairy-Free / Nut-Free

Cooking with beer is a delicate matter. Unlike wine, which is pretty much awesome in everything as far as I'm concerned, beer can be finicky. It can easily turn an entire dish bitter or yield "off" flavors, especially if you pour with a heavy hand. This beer-braised beef brisket uses just the right amount of beer to highlight the complexity of the flavors and yield tender, delicious meat.

1 tablespoon smoked
  paprika
1 tablespoon brown sugar
1 teaspoon freshly ground
  black pepper
1½ teaspoons sea salt
1 teaspoon minced
  fresh rosemary
1 tablespoon minced garlic
1 teaspoon Dijon mustard
1 tablespoon extra-virgin
  olive oil
1 (2½-pound) beef brisket
4 carrots, cut into
  2-inch pieces
2 celery stalks, cut into
  2-inch pieces
1 yellow onion, cut
  into slices
1 (12-ounce) bottle lager or
  brown ale

1. In a small bowl, combine the paprika, brown sugar, black pepper, salt, rosemary, garlic, mustard, and olive oil to make a paste. Coat the brisket evenly with the mixture.

2. Spread out the carrots, celery, and onion in the slow cooker crock.

3. Place the brisket on top of the vegetables. Pour the beer around the brisket.

4. Cover and cook on low for 8 to 10 hours.

COOKING TIP: If you have time to let the brisket soak up the rub overnight, wrap it in plastic wrap and refrigerate.

Beef and Broccoli

Prep time: **10 minutes** / Cook time: **5 to 6 hours on low, plus 2 minutes on high**
Serves: **6**
Dairy-Free / Nut-Free

Chinese takeout is a trusty standby, but it can get expensive and is often drowning in grease and MSG. The slow cooker delivers frugality and a much healthier version in this simple beef and broccoli dish. Serve over steamed rice. The only thing missing is the fortune cookie.

2 pounds sirloin steak, thinly sliced

¼ cup soy sauce

1 tablespoon rice wine vinegar

1 cup low-sodium beef broth

2 teaspoons brown sugar

3 tablespoons sesame oil

1 tablespoon minced fresh ginger

1 tablespoon minced garlic

1 teaspoon red pepper flakes

8 cups broccoli florets and stems, cut into 1-inch pieces

2 tablespoons cornstarch

1. Combine the steak, soy sauce, vinegar, beef broth, brown sugar, oil, ginger, garlic, red pepper flakes, and broccoli in the slow cooker crock. Stir gently to mix.

2. Cover and cook on low for 5 to 6 hours, until the beef and broccoli are tender.

3. Transfer the beef and broccoli to a serving dish and set aside.

4. Increase the heat to high. Transfer ¼ cup of the cooking liquid to a large measuring cup, add the cornstarch, and whisk until no lumps remain. Pour the cornstarch mixture into the slow cooker and simmer until the sauce is thickened, about 2 minutes.

5. Return the beef and broccoli and any accumulated juices to the slow cooker, stirring to coat in the sauce and serve.

INGREDIENT TIP: Boneless beef chuck will also work in this recipe.

Creamy Beef Stroganoff

Prep time: **10 minutes** / Cook time: **5 to 6 hours on low, plus 2 minutes** / Serves: **6 to 8**
Nut-Free

Many slow cooker beef stroganoff recipes call for canned soup, but I prefer to make the sauce from scratch with fresh ingredients. (The only recipe I make an exception for is Green Bean Casserole, on page 57.) I grew up with stroganoff served over pasta, but do as you wish. It's also good over potatoes or rice.

2 pounds sirloin,
  thinly sliced

2 tablespoons dry sherry

1½ cups low-sodium
  beef broth

4 tablespoons
  (½ stick) butter

2 cups halved mushrooms

1 medium yellow
  onion, minced

1 tablespoon minced garlic

1 tablespoon minced
  fresh thyme

Sea salt

Freshly ground black pepper

4 ounces cream cheese

8 ounces full-fat sour cream

16 ounces egg noodles,
  cooked according to
  package instructions,
  for serving

½ cup minced fresh
  parsley, for serving

1. Combine the steak, sherry, beef broth, butter, mushrooms, onion, garlic, and thyme in the slow cooker crock. Season generously with salt and pepper, and stir to mix.

2. Cover and cook on low for 5 to 6 hours, until the beef is tender.

3. Stir in the cream cheese and sour cream.

4. Simmer uncovered for about 2 minutes until heated through. Serve over the egg noodles and top with fresh parsley.

COOKING TIP: Want to really amp up the flavor? Stir in 2 tablespoons of beef demi-glace at the beginning of the cooking time. Demi-glace is reduced beef stock, vegetables, and wine and is available in specialty markets.

Classic Meatloaf

Prep time: **10 minutes** / Cook time: **6 to 8 hours on low** / Serves: **6 to 8**
Dairy-Free / Nut-Free

Meatloaf has enjoyed a resurgence in popularity. During the Great Depression, it was a frugal way to extend food budgets and became a trusty comfort food. It lost its luster in culinary circles for a few decades in favor of fancier fare. But now that comfort food is cool again, meatloaf, gourmet mac and cheese, and other classics are back on the menu. This version stays true to its origins. It's simple, straightforward, and just plain delicious.

1 tablespoon extra-virgin
  olive oil
2 pounds ground beef
1 pound ground pork
1 cup panko or white
  bread crumbs
1 medium onion, minced
1 tablespoon minced garlic
¼ cup minced fresh parsley
1 teaspoon dried thyme
¾ cup ketchup
2 eggs
1½ teaspoons sea salt
Freshly ground black pepper

1. Coat the interior of the slow cooker crock with the oil, making sure to cover about two-thirds up the sides of the crock.

2. In a large bowl, combine the ground beef, ground pork, panko, onion, garlic, parsley, thyme, ketchup, eggs, salt, and as much black pepper as desired with your hands until evenly mixed. Spread out the meatloaf mixture in the slow cooker crock.

3. Cover and cook on low for 6 to 8 hours or until the meatloaf is cooked through and pulls away from the sides of the crock.

COOKING TIP: Because ketchup plays such a prominent role in this dish, look for an organic version without high-fructose corn syrup. The flavors will shine!

Sunday Pot Roast

Prep time: **10 minutes** / Cook time: **8 to 10 hours on low, plus 2 minutes on high**
Serves: **6 to 8**
Nut-Free

You can serve this pot roast whatever day you like, but Sundays work well because this recipe yields plenty of leftovers for weekly meal prepping. Use the leftovers in sandwiches, to fill burritos or enchiladas, or serve them over pasta with marinara sauce.

1 (5-pound) chuck roast

2 tablespoons olive oil

2 garlic cloves, minced

1½ teaspoons sea salt

1 tablespoon freshly ground black pepper

1 tablespoon minced fresh rosemary

1 teaspoon minced fresh thyme

1 cup low-sodium beef broth

3 tablespoons dry sherry (optional)

2 tablespoons butter, melted

2 tablespoons all-purpose flour

1. Coat the chuck roast in the oil. In a small bowl, mix together the garlic, salt, black pepper, rosemary, and thyme and rub the mixture all over the roast until well coated. Put the roast in the slow cooker crock. Add the beef broth and sherry (if using), being careful not to rinse off the seasonings.

2. Cover and cook on low for 8 to 10 hours. Transfer the roast to a cutting board and let it rest for 10 minutes before cutting into slices.

3. Increase the heat to high. In a small bowl, whisk together butter and flour to make a paste. Add the mixture to the cooking liquid in the slow cooker crock and whisk until combined. Simmer for another 2 minutes, until the gravy is thickened. Serve the gravy on the side.

COOKING TIP: I keep a bottle of dry sherry in my cupboard for cooking. It adds a layer of nuttiness and complexity that I don't get from white or red wine.

Tender Beef Ragu

Prep time: 15 minutes / Cook time: **10 hours on low** / Serves: **6 to 8**
Dairy-Free / Nut-Free

I spent years following a low-ish carb diet. But in the end, love won. And I love pasta. I'll bet you do, too. The challenge is that pasta cooks in an instant, but a good sauce can take hours to cook and develop its flavors. That's where this tender beef ragu comes in. It simmers all day in a rich sauce of plum tomatoes, rosemary, thyme, and red wine. When you're ready to eat, just bring a pot of water to boil, add the pasta, and you can have dinner on the table in under 15 minutes.

2 pounds beef chuck

1 (28-ounce) can plum
  tomatoes

1 medium yellow
  onion, minced

1 carrot, diced

1 celery stalk, diced

6 garlic cloves, peeled
  and smashed

2 rosemary sprigs,
  leaves minced

4 thyme sprigs,
  leaves minced

1 teaspoon sea salt

1 teaspoon freshly ground
  black pepper

2 cups full-bodied red
  wine, such as cabernet
  or Chianti

16 ounces pasta, cooked,
  for serving

Crunchy artisan bread
  (optional)

1. Combine the beef, tomatoes, onion, carrot, celery, garlic, rosemary, thyme, salt, black pepper, and wine in the slow cooker crock. Stir to mix.

2. Cover and cook on low for 10 hours, until the beef is very tender.

3. Using two forks or meat claws, shred the meat. Taste, and adjust the seasoning, if desired. Serve over pasta alongside crunchy artisan bread (if using).

COOKING TIP: Don't have 10 hours to make this recipe? Cook it on high for 2 hours, then lower the heat to low for 6 hours for a total cook time of 8 hours.

Spicy Mediterranean Beef with Pearl Barley

Prep time: **10 minutes** / Cook time: **8 hours on low** / Serves: **6 to 8**
Dairy-Free / Nut-Free

Tomato paste, beef broth, red wine, and beef chuck cook alongside creamy pearl barley, infusing it with flavor in this hearty one-pot meal. Serve with crusty bread and a glass of Italian or Spanish red wine.

1 (4-ounce) can
  tomato paste
½ teaspoon red
  pepper flakes
2 cups low-sodium
  beef broth
2 tablespoons extra-virgin
  olive oil
1 cup dry red wine
1 cup pearl barley
2 pounds beef chuck, cut
  into 4-inch pieces
Sea salt
Freshly ground black pepper
2 red bell peppers,
  thinly sliced
1 red onion, halved and
  thinly sliced

1. Combine the tomato paste, red pepper flakes, beef broth, olive oil, and wine in the slow cooker crock. Whisk until mixed. Stir in the barley.

2. Lay the beef chuck over the barley and season generously with salt and black pepper.

3. Spread out the peppers and onion around the beef.

4. Cover and cook on low for 8 hours, until the barley and beef are very tender.

INGREDIENT TIP: For a whole-grain option, choose hulled barley, which has had just the outer husk removed. No need to adjust the cooking time.

Red Miso Beef

Prep time: **10 minutes** / Cook time: **8 to 10 hours on low** / Serves: **6 to 8**
Dairy-Free / Gluten-Free / Nut-Free

This recipe is adapted from one of my favorite restaurants in Los Angeles: Lemonade. This dish is sweet and savory and has loads of umami flavors from the miso. If you can't find red miso, regular white miso will work fine. The original recipe calls for beef short ribs. While they're tasty, they're also somewhat expensive and require searing before adding to the slow cooker. Instead, I use brisket, which is a proximal cut of boneless beef.

1 (3-pound) beef brisket, cut into 4-inch pieces
1 medium yellow onion, diced
4 garlic cloves, peeled and smashed
1 tablespoon minced fresh ginger
2 teaspoons ground allspice
½ cup apple cider vinegar
1 (4-ounce) can tomato paste
½ cup molasses
2 tablespoons chili garlic sauce
2 cups low-sodium beef broth
½ cup red or white miso (check label for gluten-free)
2 scallions, thinly sliced
2 tablespoons sesame seeds

1. Put the beef, onion, garlic, ginger, allspice, vinegar, tomato paste, molasses, chili garlic sauce, and beef broth in the slow cooker crock.

2. Cover and cook on low for 8 to 10 hours, until the beef is very tender.

3. Transfer the beef to a serving platter.

4. Whisk the miso into the slow cooker juices and mix until dissolved. Pour the sauce over the beef and top with the scallions and sesame seeds.

INGREDIENT TIP: Miso has live active cultures (like yogurt or kombucha) that are sensitive to heat. To keep them active, I add the miso after the full cooking time.

Beef Bourguignon

Prep time: **10 minutes** / Cook time: **8 hours on low, plus 12 minutes on high**
Serves: **6 to 8**
Nut-Free

I learned to make beef bourguignon while living in Europe and going through a phase of devouring everything Julia Child had written, including of course, *Mastering the Art of French Cooking*. What really stood out to me is how few ingredients her recipes call for. Sometimes the simplest recipe is also the best. This slow-cooker version provides an easy on-ramp to French cooking.

3 pounds beef stew meat, cut into 2-inch pieces

1 teaspoon sea salt

1 teaspoon freshly ground black pepper

2 cups light-bodied dry red wine, such as pinot noir

2 cups low-sodium beef broth

1 tablespoon tomato paste

2 carrots, diced

8 ounces frozen pearl onions, thawed

2 thyme sprigs

1 rosemary sprig

2 tablespoons butter, melted

2 tablespoons all-purpose flour

¼ cup minced fresh parsley

1. Put the beef, salt, black pepper, wine, beef broth, tomato paste, carrots, onions, thyme, and rosemary in the slow cooker crock.

2. Cover and cook on low for 8 hours, until the beef is tender.

3. Transfer the beef to a serving dish, cover, and set aside.

4. Increase the heat to high and simmer for another 10 minutes until slightly reduced. Remove the thyme and rosemary sprigs and discard.

5. In a small bowl, whisk together the melted butter and flour to make a paste. Whisk the flour mixture into the crock and cook until just thickened, about another 2 minutes.

6. Pour the sauce over the beef, garnish with the parsley, and serve.

COOKING TIP: For a more flavorful version, sear the beef before adding it to the stew. Season with salt and pepper and coat in the flour, shaking off any excess. Sear the meat in a hot skillet over medium-high heat with 1 tablespoon of canola oil, turning frequently, until browned on all sides. Transfer the meat to the slow cooker. Deglaze the skillet with ¼ cup of the wine, scraping up all of the browned bits, then pour the liquid into the crock. Proceed with the recipe as written, stirring in the butter alone in step 5.

Barbacoa

Prep time: **10 minutes** / Cook time: **8 to 10 hours on low** / Serves: **6 to 8**
Dairy-Free / Gluten-Free

This dish is traditionally cooked overnight in a big hole in the ground. I don't know about you, but I don't have a cooking pit in my backyard. But I do have a preferred method for cooking low and slow—no surprise here, it's the slow cooker! Although the method is different, the ingredients are classic.

1 medium yellow onion,
    cut into wedges
2 guajillo chiles, stems
    removed
6 garlic cloves, peeled
    and smashed
1 teaspoon dried oregano
1 teaspoon ground cumin
1 teaspoon sea salt
1 teaspoon freshly ground
    black pepper
2 cups water
2½ pounds beef brisket, cut
    into 6 to 8 pieces
Corn tortillas, for serving
Cilantro-Onion Salsa
    (page 107, step 5)

1. Put the onion, chiles, garlic, oregano, cumin, salt, black pepper, and water into a blender and puree until smooth.

2. Pour mixture from the blender into the slow cooker crock. Add the brisket and turn it to coat it in the sauce.

3. Cover and cook on low for 8 to 10 hours, until the meat is very tender.

4. Using two forks or meat claws, shred the meat. Serve in corn tortillas and top with the cilantro-onion salsa.

COOKING TIP: For truly authentic barbacoa, sear the onion and toast the chiles before adding them to the blender. Also, fry the prepared barbacoa in a hot skillet with 1 tablespoon of oil before serving it in the tortillas.

Sloppy Joes

Prep time: **10 minutes** / Cook time: **8 to 10 hours on low** / Serves: **6 to 8**
Dairy-Free / Gluten-Free / Nut-Free

I wanted to call this "pulled beef" because that sounds so much fancier than "sloppy joes." But sometimes you just want comfort food without pretense. And that's what this recipe delivers. It's simple, easy, and so much healthier and tastier than anything you could get from a can.

3 pounds beef chuck

1 (16-ounce) bottle barbecue sauce (check label for gluten-free)

1 tablespoon smoked paprika

1 medium yellow onion, halved and thinly sliced

4 garlic cloves, minced

1 teaspoon freshly ground black pepper

1 cup low-sodium beef broth

1. Put the beef, barbecue sauce, paprika, onion, garlic, black pepper, and beef broth in the slow cooker crock.

2. Cover and cook on low for 8 to 10 hours, until the meat is falling apart. Using two forks or meat claws, shred the meat.

INGREDIENT TIP: Use a good-quality barbecue sauce without high-fructose corn syrup.

Italian Sausage and Peppers

Prep time: **10 minutes** / Cook time: **6 to 8 hours on low** / Serves: **8**
Dairy-Free / Nut-Free

These spicy Italian sausages and peppers fill hoagie rolls and are perfect for tailgating. Use a good-quality marinara sauce in this recipe. It really will make a huge difference. See the tip following the recipe for more on how to pick a good sauce.

2 pounds spicy or sweet
   Italian sausages
2 medium yellow onions,
   halved and thinly sliced
2 red bell peppers,
   thinly sliced
2 green bell peppers,
   thinly sliced
¼ teaspoon red
   pepper flakes
1 teaspoon fennel seeds,
   smashed
8 garlic cloves, peeled and
   smashed
1 (24-ounce) jar
   marinara sauce
8 hoagie rolls

1. Put the sausages, onions, red and green bell peppers, red pepper flakes, fennel, garlic, and marinara sauce in the slow cooker.

2. Cover and cook on low for 6 to 8 hours, until the sausages are cooked through and the vegetables are tender.

3. Serve the sausages in the hoagie rolls and top with the onions and peppers.

INGREDIENT TIP: How can you tell if a premade marinara sauce is good quality? Look for sauces with a few simple ingredients, such as tomatoes, garlic, olive oil, salt, and basil. Good sauce should not contain tomato concentrate or high-fructose corn syrup. Price is a fair indication of quality, too. A sauce that's double the price of lower-priced items is, in my experience, twice as good.

Chile Verde Pork

Prep time: **10 minutes** / Cook time: **8 to 10 hours on low** / Serves: **6 to 8**
Dairy-Free / Gluten-Free / Nut-Free

Salsa verde is a blend of roasted tomatillos, onion, garlic, and chile peppers. It is tangy and complex. Although you can make the salsa at home, starting with a quality store-bought version will save you half an hour of cooking and prep time. Serve the pork and peppers over rice or shred it and use it in tacos or enchiladas.

1 tablespoon canola oil
1 (2½-pound) pork butt (also called pork shoulder)
Sea salt
Freshly ground black pepper
1 tablespoon ground cumin
1 yellow onion, halved and thinly sliced
2 green bell peppers, thinly sliced
2 poblano peppers, thinly sliced
1 (16-ounce) jar salsa verde
¼ cup minced fresh cilantro

1. Coat the interior of the slow cooker with the oil, making sure to cover about two-thirds up the sides of the crock.

2. Season the pork generously with salt, black pepper, and the cumin.

3. Spread out the onion, bell peppers, and poblanos in the crock and place the pork on top. Pour the salsa verde over the pork.

4. Cover and cook on low for 8 to 10 hours, until the meat is cooked to an internal temperature of 145°F.

5. Transfer the pork to a cutting board and let it rest for 15 minutes. Using two forks or meat claws, shred the meat. Garnish with the fresh cilantro.

VARIATION TIP: This recipe can also be made with bone-in, skinless chicken thighs. Use 2½ pounds and cook for 6 to 8 hours.

Sage and Lemon Braised Pork

Prep time: **5 minutes** / Cook time: **8 to 10 hours on low, plus 15 minutes on high**
Serves: **6 to 8**
Dairy-Free

Sage, garlic, and lemon infuse pork butt with flavor as it cooks in a shallow braise of almond milk. That might sound like a strange braising liquid, but it accentuates the natural flavors of the pork. The orzo makes this a nicely balanced one-dish meal. It soaks up all of the delicious juices from the cooked meat—just don't add it until the end of the cooking time or it will be mushy.

1 (2½- to 3-pound) pork butt (also called pork shoulder)
1 tablespoon extra-virgin olive oil
1 teaspoon sea salt
1 teaspoon freshly ground black pepper
2 sage sprigs, minced
1 teaspoon minced garlic
Zest of 1 lemon
2 cups unsweetened almond milk
1½ cups orzo pasta

1. Coat the pork with the olive oil, then rub the salt, black pepper, sage, garlic, and lemon zest on it.

2. Pour the almond milk into the slow cooker crock. Add the pork.

3. Cover and cook on low for 8 to 10 hours, until the pork is cooked through to an internal temperature of 145°F. Transfer the pork to a cutting board and let it rest for 15 minutes before cutting it into slices.

4. Add the orzo to the cooking liquid in the crock, cover, increase the heat to high, and simmer for 15 minutes, until all of the liquid is absorbed.

COOKING TIP: Because this is a larger cut of meat, using an instant-read meat thermometer is the easiest way to determine doneness.

Pork Shoulder with Chimichurri

Prep time: **10 minutes** / Cook time: **8 to 10 hours on low** / Serves: **6 to 8**
Dairy-Free / Gluten-Free / Nut-Free

Chimichurri might be my favorite sauce. It's bright and punchy and livens up everything from grilled vegetables to meat, especially when you're cooking in a slow cooker, where flavors might dull after hours of cooking. In this recipe, it does double duty, serving both as a flavor booster during cooking and a condiment at the dinner table.

1 bunch fresh parsley

1 bunch fresh cilantro

1 tablespoon dried oregano

4 garlic cloves, peeled

Zest and juice of 1 lime

2 tablespoons apple
  cider vinegar

½ cup extra-virgin olive oil,
  plus 1 tablespoon

1 teaspoon sea salt

1 teaspoon freshly ground
  black pepper

1 (2½- to 3-pound)
  pork butt (also called
  pork shoulder)

1. Combine the parsley, cilantro, oregano, garlic, lime zest and juice, vinegar, ½ cup of olive oil, salt, and black pepper in a blender, and blend until mostly smooth. Set aside.

2. Coat the interior of the slow cooker crock with the remaining 1 tablespoon of oil.

3. Put the pork butt in the crock. Pour about half of the chimichurri sauce over the pork. Refrigerate the remaining chimichurri.

4. Cover and cook on low for 8 to 10 hours, or until the meat is cooked to an internal temperature of 145°F.

5. Let the meat rest for 15 minutes, then cut it into slices and serve with the remaining chimichurri on the side.

VARIATION TIP: Certain people have a genetic predisposition to dislike the taste of cilantro. If you're among them, use two bunches of parsley in this recipe and double the amount of oregano.

Carnitas Street Tacos

Prep time: **10 minutes** / Cook time: **8 hours on low** / Serves: **6 to 8**
Dairy-Free / Gluten-Free

The tacos I grew up with were as American as it gets—large flour tortillas filled with ground beef seasoned from a packet and topped with shredded lettuce, cheese, and tomatoes. A classic. But hardly related to the street tacos of Central America where carnitas fill small corn tortillas that fit in the palm of your hand. In this version, like in authentic tacos, the toppings are sparse but flavorful—just bits of onion, jalapeño, cilantro, and lime juice.

1 teaspoon extra-virgin
 olive oil
Zest and juice of 1 orange
Zest and juice of 1 lime
1 tablespoon minced garlic
1 tablespoon ground cumin
1 teaspoon ground coriander
1 cup Low-Sodium Chicken
 Broth (page 124),
 or store-bought
Sea salt
Freshly ground black pepper
1 (2-pound) pork butt (also
 called pork shoulder)
1 small yellow onion,
 finely diced
¼ cup minced fresh cilantro
1 small jalapeño
 pepper, minced
Juice of 1 lime
16 small corn tortillas,
 for serving

1. Coat the interior of the slow cooker crock with the oil, making sure to cover about two-thirds up the side of the crock.

2. In a small bowl, whisk together the orange zest and juice, lime zest and juice, garlic, cumin, coriander, and chicken broth. Season with salt and black pepper.

3. Put the pork in the slow cooker crock. Pour the orange juice mixture over the pork.

4. Cover and cook on low for 8 hours. Let the meat rest for 15 minutes before using two forks or meat claws to shred it.

5. While the carnitas cook, make the cilantro-onion salsa. In a bowl, combine the onion, cilantro, jalapeño, and lime juice.

TO ASSEMBLE THE TACOS

6. Optional: Fry the carnitas in small batches in a large skillet coated with canola oil over medium-high heat until crispy and browned on the edges, 3 to 4 minutes.

7. Serve in corn tortillas topped with the salsa.

STORAGE TIP: Store leftover meat in a covered container in the refrigerator for up to 3 days or in the freezer for up to 3 months.

Peachy Balsamic Pork Tenderloin

Prep time: **15 minutes** / Cook time: **5 to 6 hours on low, plus 15 minutes on high**
Serves: **6**
Dairy-Free / Gluten-Free / Nut-Free

Fresh, sweet, juicy peaches meld with fresh rosemary and red onion to make a delicious condiment for pork, all in one pot. The sauce is similar in texture to a chutney but has a more familiar and subtle flavor that will delight kids and adults alike. Make this recipe in the summertime when peaches are at their peak and you want to leave the oven off.

1 tablespoon canola oil

4 cups peeled sliced peaches

1 tablespoon minced fresh rosemary

1 medium red onion, halved and thinly sliced

1 garlic clove, peeled and smashed

¼ cup balsamic vinegar

½ cup Low-Sodium Chicken Broth (page 124), or store-bought

2 (1½-pound) pork tenderloins

Sea salt

Freshly ground black pepper

2 tablespoons brown sugar

1. Coat the interior of the slow cooker crock with the oil, making sure to cover about two-thirds up the sides of the crock.

2. Spread out the peaches, rosemary, onion, and garlic in the crock. Pour in the vinegar and chicken broth.

3. Place the pork on top of the peach mixture and season generously with salt and black pepper.

4. Cover and cook on low for 5 to 6 hours, until the meat is cooked to an internal temperature of 145°F. Remove it from the slow cooker and transfer it to a cutting board. Let the meat rest for 15 minutes before cutting it into slices.

5. Stir the brown sugar into the peach sauce, increase the temperature to high, and simmer uncovered until the liquid reduces and the sauce is thick and sticky, about 15 minutes. Serve the sauce alongside the pork.

INGREDIENT TIP: If you prefer to use frozen peaches, thaw them in the refrigerator overnight before adding them to the slow cooker. You may need to increase the brown sugar by 1 tablespoon if the peaches are not particularly sweet. Do not use canned peaches.

Lamb Tagine

Prep time: **10 minutes** / Cook time: **8 to 10 hours on low** / Serves: **6 to 8**
Dairy-Free / Gluten-Free

Tagine is a traditional Moroccan dish that is both a stew and the pot in which it's slowly cooked over low heat. Although the slow cooker isn't the traditional vessel, it does replicate the low-and-slow cooking method and results in the classic flavors. This version includes ingredients common in Moroccan tagine, such as ginger, turmeric, dried fruit, and almonds. The sweet spices balance the somewhat grassy, gamey flavor of the lamb.

1 medium yellow
  onion, diced
2 carrots, diced
2 celery stalks, diced
½ cup sliced dried apricots
1 tablespoon minced ginger
1 tablespoon ground cumin
1 tablespoon ground
  turmeric
¼ teaspoon ground
  cinnamon
½ teaspoon cayenne pepper
2 teaspoons sea salt
2 tablespoons brown sugar
½ cup sliced dried figs
½ cup toasted slivered
  almonds
2 pounds boneless lamb
  shoulder, cut into
  1-inch cubes
Freshly ground black pepper
4 cups Low-Sodium
  Chicken Broth (page 124),
  or store-bought

1. Combine the onion, carrot, celery, apricots, ginger, cumin, turmeric, cinnamon, cayenne pepper, salt, brown sugar, figs, almonds, lamb, black pepper, and chicken broth in the slow cooker crock. Stir to mix.

2. Cover and cook on low for 8 to 10 hours, or until the lamb is tender.

VARIATION TIP: If you cannot find lamb or don't like how it tastes, you can use beef chuck instead.

Peanut Butter Chocolate Cake, page 112

CHAPTER 8

Desserts

Peanut Butter Chocolate Cake

Prep time: **10 minutes** / Cook time: **3 hours on low** / Serves: **6 to 8**
Vegetarian

This cake is as decadent as it sounds. Creamy peanut butter and butterscotch chips form ribbons of salty, nutty flavor throughout a chocolate cake. I debated whether to use a boxed mix or provide a recipe to make it from scratch, but the whole point of a slow cooker is to make your life easier. Save the homemade chocolate cake for those moments when you have plenty of time and can use the oven.

1 tablespoon butter
1 box chocolate cake mix
3 eggs
½ cup oil
1¼ cups water
1 cup butterscotch chips
1 cup creamy peanut butter
½ cup milk

1. Coat the interior of the slow cooker crock with the butter, making sure to cover about two-thirds up the sides of the crock.

2. In a separate bowl, whisk together the cake mix, eggs, oil, and water. Pour the mixture into the slow cooker crock.

3. Sprinkle the butterscotch chips over the surface of the cake batter.

4. In the same bowl you used to mix the cake batter, combine the peanut butter and milk.

5. Top the cake batter with spoonfuls of the peanut butter mixture, dropping each spoonful a few inches apart. Use a knife to swirl the peanut butter mixture, incorporating the butterscotch chips as you go. Make sure not to thoroughly mix. You still want a distinct peanut butter swirl.

6. Cover and cook on low for 3 hours, until set.

VARIATION TIP: If you can't find butterscotch chips, you can omit them or replace them with dark chocolate chips. For an entirely different twist, replace the peanut butter with raspberry jam, replace the milk with water, and replace the butterscotch chips with white chocolate chips for a raspberry and white chocolate swirl cake.

Chocolate Lava Cake

Prep time: **10 minutes** / Cook time: **3 hours 30 minutes on high** / Serves: **8 to 10**
Nut-Free / Vegetarian

There's a scene in the movie *Chef* in which Jon Favreau lights into a restaurant critic who incorrectly asserts that chocolate lava cake is merely underdone chocolate cake. "That's not what makes the center molten!" he seethes. In restaurant versions, it's made by freezing a cylinder of ganache and placing it in the center of each ramekin. In this slow cooker version, we'll pour the ganache right over the top of the cake to create that ooey-gooey texture without risking underdone batter.

1 tablespoon butter

1 box chocolate cake mix

3 eggs

½ cup oil

2 teaspoons vanilla extract

1½ cups water

1 (4-ounce) package instant chocolate pudding mix

2 cups whole milk

1 tablespoon instant coffee powder (optional)

1 (11-ounce) bag 60 percent cacao chocolate chips

1. Coat the interior of the slow cooker crock with the butter, making sure to cover about two-thirds up the sides of the crock.

2. In a large bowl, whisk together the cake mix, eggs, oil, vanilla, and water. Pour the mixture into the slow cooker crock.

3. In the same bowl you used to mix the cake batter, whisk together the pudding mix, milk, and instant coffee powder. Pour this mixture over the chocolate cake mix. Top with the chocolate chips.

4. Cover and cook on high for 3 hours and 30 minutes, until set in the center.

INGREDIENT TIP: Use a chocolate fudge or devil's food cake mix for the best results.

Pumpkin Spice Dump Cake

Prep time: **10 minutes** / Cook time: **4 hours on low** / Serves: **6 to 8**
Nut-Free / Vegetarian

This pumpkin spice dump cake marries the flavors of two classic desserts, pumpkin pie and cobbler, to create a sweetly spiced, dense filling beneath a crumbly topping. Try serving this dessert on holidays when you want homemade pie but don't quite have the time to make one from scratch. Serve with whipped cream.

1 tablespoon unsalted butter, plus ½ cup melted

1 (15-ounce) can pumpkin puree

1 cup whole milk

2 eggs, beaten

¾ cup brown sugar

1 tablespoon pumpkin pie spice

1 teaspoon vanilla extract

1 box yellow cake mix

1. Coat the interior of the slow cooker crock with 1 tablespoon of butter, making sure to cover about two-thirds up the sides of the crock.

2. In the slow cooker crock, whisk together the pumpkin, milk, eggs, brown sugar, pumpkin pie spice, and vanilla until just combined.

3. In a separate bowl, combine the remaining ½ cup of melted butter and cake mix until crumbly. Spread the cake mixture over the pumpkin mixture in the slow cooker crock.

4. Cover the crock with a clean tea towel, then top with the lid. Cook on low for 4 hours. Let the cake cool to room temperature before serving.

COOKING TIP: The tea towel will capture any condensation that otherwise would have fallen onto the topping. Paper towels are acceptable, too.

Butterscotch Pudding

Prep time: **10 minutes** / Cook time: **2 to 3 hours on high** / Serves: **6 to 8**
Nut-Free / Vegetarian

I debated whether to call this a pudding or a cake. In the United Kingdom, it would fall decidedly into the pudding camp. In fact, one of the essential ingredients in this dish is golden syrup, also known as light treacle in England. Don't worry, you can find it at most big box stores or online. Whether you call it pudding or cake, this dessert is deliciously messy and best served in bowls with a generous scoop of vanilla ice cream.

1 tablespoon butter, plus
⅓ cup softened
3 cups all-purpose flour
1 tablespoon baking powder
1½ cups brown sugar
1½ cups whole milk
½ teaspoon sea salt
½ cup golden syrup
1 cup hot water
Vanilla ice cream, for serving

1. Coat the interior of the slow cooker crock with 1 tablespoon of butter, making sure to cover about two-thirds up the sides of the crock.

2. In a large bowl, whisk together the flour, baking powder, brown sugar, milk, and salt until well combined. Pour the batter into the crock.

3. In a separate bowl, whisk together the remaining ⅓ cup of butter, the golden syrup, and water until the butter is melted. Carefully pour the mixture over the cake batter.

4. Cover and cook on high for 2 to 3 hours, until just set. Serve with the vanilla ice cream.

INGREDIENT TIP: Use aluminum-free baking powder for the best flavor; sometimes a faint metallic taste results from regular baking powder.

Chocolate Bread Pudding

Prep time: **10 minutes** / Cook time: **3 hours on low** / Serves: **6 to 8**
Nut-Free / Vegetarian

I usually have a bag of chocolate chips in the house. But I don't always have the time to whip up a batch of chocolate chip cookies. This bread pudding hits many of those same notes—chocolatey, sweet, and with a hint of salt. It also reminds me of the French pastry pain au chocolat but with half the effort.

1 tablespoon butter

8 cups cubed bread, ideally day-old French bread

2 cups whole milk

½ cup heavy (whipping) cream

2 eggs, beaten

1 tablespoon vanilla extract

2 cups chocolate chips

1. Coat the interior of the slow cooker crock with the butter, making sure to cover about two-thirds up the sides of the crock.

2. Put the bread in the slow cooker crock.

3. In a separate bowl, whisk together the milk, cream, eggs, and vanilla. Pour the mixture over the bread in the slow cooker crock. Stir gently to mix. Let it rest for about 5 minutes to allow the bread to soak up the milk mixture.

4. Stir in the chocolate chips, making sure they are distributed evenly.

5. Cover and cook on low for 3 hours, until set.

INGREDIENT TIP: The best bread for this recipe is one with a little texture. A baguette is your best bet because it has lots of crust. That keeps the pudding from getting too mushy or feeling like it has a homogenous texture.

Spiced Rum and Raisin Rice Pudding

Prep time: **5 minutes** / Cook time: **4 hours on low** / Serves: **8**
Dairy-Free / Gluten-Free / Nut-Free / Vegan

As a child, I didn't appreciate the subtlety of rice pudding. It wasn't quite sweet enough, and I couldn't figure out why anyone would want rice for dessert. As an adult, I now get it—the subtle sweetness of the coconut milk and cinnamon-infused rice is plenty indulgent. It's just as well then to spike it with a little rum and save this dessert for adult palates. That said, most of the alcohol cooks off, so it's probably fine to serve to the little ones.

1 tablespoon vegan butter
    or regular butter

2 cups short-grain white rice

2 teaspoons ground
    cinnamon

2 (14-ounce) cans full-fat
    coconut milk, plus more
    if desired

¼ cup spiced dark rum

¾ cup brown sugar

¼ teaspoon sea salt

1 tablespoon vanilla extract

1 cup raisins

1 cup water

1. Coat the interior of the slow cooker crock with the butter, making sure to cover about two-thirds up the sides of the crock.

2. Put the rice, cinnamon, coconut milk, rum, brown sugar, salt, vanilla, raisins, and water in the crock. Stir gently to mix.

3. Cover and cook on low for 4 hours, until the rice is tender. Stir in additional coconut milk or water to thin the pudding to your desired consistency.

VARIATION TIP: You can make this with whole milk if you prefer it to coconut milk and water.

Mulled Wine–Poached Pears

Prep time: **10 minutes** / Cook time: **4 hours on low** / Serves: **6 to 8**
Dairy-Free / Gluten-Free / Nut-Free / Vegan

Mulled wine holds a special place in my heart. I went to Germany for Christmas one year to spend the holiday with my husband's family. We enjoyed a Christmas market where every other vendor, it seemed, served mulled wine and sausages. I enjoyed a steaming mug under a lightly falling snow while a brass band played. It was idyllic.

1 (750-ml) bottle fruity red wine, such as zinfandel

½ cup sugar

¼ cup brandy (optional)

1 orange, cut into slices

2 cinnamon sticks

8 ripe pears, peeled and cut into slices

Vanilla ice cream, for serving

1. Combine the wine, sugar, and brandy (if using) in the slow cooker crock. Stir until the sugar is at least partially dissolved.

2. Add the sliced orange, cinnamon, and pears. Stir gently to mix.

3. Cover and cook on low for 4 hours, until the pears are very tender.

4. Transfer the pears to individual serving dishes. Serve with the vanilla ice cream.

SERVING TIP: Serve the mulled wine that remains in the slow cooker as a beverage. The alcohol content will be somewhat reduced.

Berry Cobbler

Prep time: **10 minutes** / Cook time: **4 hours on low or 2 hours on high** / Serves: **6 to 8**
Nut-Free / Vegetarian

I grew up picking fresh blackberries and blueberries with my mom in the Pacific Northwest. I never realized how lucky I was to have fresh berries so readily available until I moved away. If, like me these days, you're not so close to a berry patch, frozen berries work just as well. See the tip following the recipe for how to use them.

8 cups fresh or frozen assorted berries, such as strawberries, blueberries, and blackberries
2 tablespoons cornstarch
1 tablespoon lemon juice
½ cup sugar
1 (16-ounce) package refrigerated biscuits
Whipped cream or vanilla ice cream, for serving

1. Combine the berries, cornstarch, lemon juice, and sugar in the slow cooker crock. Stir the mixture until the berries are well coated in the cornstarch.

2. Arrange the biscuits over the berry mixture.

3. Cover and cook on low for 4 hours or on high for 2 hours. Serve with the whipped cream.

INGREDIENT TIP: If you're using frozen berries, do not thaw them before adding to this recipe. Because the berries are not highly perishable, they'll be fine coming up to temperature slowly in the slow cooker. You'll just need to add 30 minutes to the cooking time.

Apple Pie Filling

Prep time: **10 minutes** / Cook time: **6 hours on low** / Serves: **6 to 8**
Gluten-Free / Nut-Free / Vegetarian

Even before I married my husband, I had heard about his mother's apple pie. They called it the "magnum opus." Its crust towered over the pie dish, filled with a mountain of apples. As the years passed, my life became busier, and I didn't have the time to roll out a double crust. As a result, the pie became a distant memory. Thankfully, I have my slow cooker, which cuts the prep time in half and gives me all of the cinnamony goodness of the original.

8 tart apples, such as Granny Smith or Pink Lady, peeled, cored, and cut into slices

1½ teaspoons ground cinnamon

¼ teaspoon ground nutmeg

¼ teaspoon sea salt

4 tablespoons (½ stick) cold butter, cut into pieces

1 tablespoon all-purpose flour or gluten-free flour

½ cup brown sugar

1. Put the apples, cinnamon, nutmeg, salt, butter, flour, and brown sugar in the slow cooker crock. Stir gently to mix.

2. Cover and cook on low for 6 hours, until the apples are very tender.

VARIATION TIP: Make this into a pie by adding a store-bought pie crust. Cut the dough to fit the slow cooker and place it on top of the filling. Cover and cook as instructed.

Pumpkin Butter

Prep time: **10 minutes** / Cook time: **5 to 6 hours on low** / Serves: **8**
Dairy-Free / Gluten-Free / Nut-Free / Vegan

The flavors of pumpkin pie meet apple butter in this creamy dessert. Serve it as a topping for ice cream or as a dollop on French toast. It's also super yummy paired with hard cheeses and crackers.

2 (28-ounce) cans
  pumpkin puree
2 cups unfiltered apple cider
1½ cups brown sugar
1 teaspoon ground cinnamon
1 teaspoon ground ginger
1 teaspoon ground nutmeg
¼ teaspoon sea salt

1. Combine the pumpkin puree, apple cider, brown sugar, cinnamon, ginger, nutmeg, and salt in the slow cooker crock. Stir gently to mix.

2. Cover and cook on low for 5 to 6 hours, stirring once or twice, until it is very thick and flavorful.

INGREDIENT TIP: If you use nutmeg infrequently, as most of us do, buy a jar of whole nutmeg and grate just what you need using a fine grater. I have been using the same jar for the last 8 years, and it's just as tasty now as it was when I bought it.

Mulled Cider, page 131

Sauces and Staples

Low-Sodium Chicken Broth

Prep time: **10 minutes** / Cook time: **8 to 10 hours on low** / Serves: **6 to 8**
Dairy-Free / Gluten-Free / Nut-Free

This recipe does double duty. It yields 4 quarts of flavorful chicken broth and a couple pounds of cooked chicken that you can use for casseroles, enchiladas, soups, sandwiches, or wherever else you use cooked chicken.

1 whole 3-pound chicken, skin removed
1 medium onion, cut into thick rings
2 carrots, halved
2 celery stalks, halved
1 handful fresh parsley
4 garlic cloves, peeled and smashed
1 teaspoon peppercorns
1 bay leaf
1 teaspoon sea salt
4 quarts cold water

1. Put the chicken, onion, carrots, celery, parsley, garlic, peppercorns, bay leaf, salt, and water in the slow cooker crock. Stir to mix.

2. Cover and cook on low for 8 to 10 hours, until the chicken is cooked through. Transfer the chicken to a separate dish.

3. Strain the broth and discard the solids. Use immediately or cool, cover, and refrigerate for up to 4 days, or freeze for up to 2 months.

VARIATION TIP: If you don't care to prepare a whole chicken, you can also use the carcass of a rotisserie chicken or a pound or two of leftover chicken bones. The broth will be ready in 6 to 8 hours.

Vegetable Broth

Prep time: **10 minutes** / Cook time: **4 hours on low** / Serves: **6 to 8**
Dairy-Free / Gluten-Free / Nut-Free / Vegan

I'll let you in on a little secret. I rarely use fresh veggies to make my vegetable broth. Instead, I save scraps for a few weeks in the freezer. A top of an onion here. The end of a carrot there. Herb scraps along the way. The ingredients below call for fresh vegetables, but if you plan ahead, the scraps will work just as well. Use a rough estimate to make sure you have about the same volume as called for below. This isn't an exact science though, so don't fret if you're missing one ingredient or only have a small amount of it.

1 medium onion, cut
 into quarters
4 celery stalks, halved
4 carrots, halved
4 garlic cloves, peeled
 and smashed
1 tomato, halved
Handful fresh parsley
4 thyme sprigs
1 teaspoon
 black peppercorns
1 teaspoon sea salt
6 quarts cold water

1. Put the onion, celery, carrots, garlic, tomato, parsley, thyme, peppercorns, salt, and water in the slow cooker crock. Stir to mix.

2. Cover and cook on low for 4 hours. Taste, and adjust the seasoning, if desired.

3. Strain the broth and discard the solids. Use immediately or cool, cover, and refrigerate for up to 4 days, or freeze for up to 2 months.

INGREDIENT TIP: Here are a few other optional ingredients that will add flavor and body to your vegetable broth: mushroom stems, pieces of green or red bell pepper, or a Parmesan rind.

Marinara Sauce

Prep time: **10 minutes** / Cook time: **4 to 6 hours on low** / Serves: **6 to 8**
Dairy-Free / Gluten-Free / Nut-Free / Vegan

I never understood how delicious homemade marinara sauce was until I made it from scratch with fresh tomatoes for the first time. The secret lies in its simplicity—just tomatoes, olive oil, garlic, salt, and basil. That's it! Here's the thing, make sure you're using really good-quality tomatoes when they're in season. If you can afford to buy organic or shop at a farmers' market, go for it. Or better yet, grow them yourself.

6 pounds fresh
  tomatoes, quartered
3 garlic cloves, minced
6 fresh basil leaves
2 teaspoons sea salt
½ cup extra-virgin olive oil

1. Put the tomatoes, garlic, basil, salt, and olive oil in the slow cooker crock. Stir gently to mix.

2. Cover and cook on low for 4 to 6 hours.

3. Using an immersion blender, puree the sauce until it's mostly smooth. Use immediately or cool, cover, and refrigerate for up to 3 days.

INGREDIENT TIP: If your only option is mealy plum tomatoes in the middle of January, use 2 (28-ounce) cans of whole plum tomatoes instead.

Green Chile Cheese Sauce

Prep time: **10 minutes** / Cook time: **1 hour 30 minutes on low** / Serves: **6 to 8**
Gluten-Free / Nut-Free / Vegetarian

You don't need any excuses to make this tasty chili sauce. It's equally at home over baked potatoes or tortilla chips, and it's great on its own as a dip. Feel free to use Monterey Jack cheese instead of the pepper jack if you want to cool off the heat a bit.

8 ounces shredded pepper jack cheese

8 ounces shredded American cheese

8 ounces full-fat cream cheese, cut into 1-inch cubes

¾ cup whole milk

1 teaspoon ground cumin

1 (4-ounce) can green chiles, drained

2 scallions, thinly sliced

1 garlic clove, minced

1. Put the pepper jack, American cheese, cream cheese, milk, cumin, chiles, scallions, and garlic in the slow cooker crock. Stir to mix.

2. Cover and cook on low for 1 hour and 30 minutes, until the cheese is melted and smooth. Stir until the sauce is well blended.

COOKING TIP: Serving this queso dip at a party? Keep the slow cooker on warm to keep the sauce smooth and hot throughout the event.

Caramelized Onions

Prep time: **10 minutes** / Cook time: **8 to 10 hours on low** / Serves: **6 to 8**
Gluten-Free / Nut-Free / Vegetarian

Caramelized onions work well as a topping for burgers or pizza and, of course, as a base for onion soup. Although it takes longer to caramelize onions in the slow cooker than it does on the stovetop, it's all hands-off. So, make this big batch ahead of time and freeze the leftovers to use later. See the tip following the recipe to make onion soup.

6 large yellow onions, thinly sliced
2 tablespoons butter
2 tablespoons canola oil
1 teaspoon sugar
1 teaspoon minced fresh thyme
Sea salt

1. Put the onions, butter, oil, sugar, and thyme into the slow cooker crock. Stir gently to mix.

2. Cover and cook on high for 8 to 10 hours. Taste, and season with salt.

3. Transfer the onions to a container, cool, cover, and store for up to 3 days in the refrigerator or in the freezer for up to 1 month.

VARIATION TIP: To make this into onion soup, after cooking, increase the heat to high, stir in 2 tablespoons of brandy and cook uncovered for 2 minutes. Add 8 cups of low-sodium beef broth, cover, and simmer for another 30 minutes.

Salsa Verde

Prep time: **10 minutes** / Cook time: **6 hours on low** / Serves: **6 to 8**
Dairy-Free / Gluten-Free / Vegan

I love having salsa verde on hand to liven up soups, stews, and cooked chicken or to serve as a dip with tortilla chips. For a more authentic flavor, see the tip for instructions on how to char the peppers, tomatillos, and onion.

2 jalapeño peppers, diced
2 poblano peppers, diced
12 tomatillos, diced
1 large yellow onion, diced
8 garlic cloves, peeled
  and smashed
½ teaspoon sea salt
½ teaspoon ground cumin
¼ cup minced fresh cilantro
Juice of 1 lime

1. Put the jalapeños, poblanos, tomatillos, onion, garlic, salt, and cumin in the slow cooker crock. Stir to mix.

2. Cover and cook on low for 6 hours, or until the sauce is thick and the vegetables are nearly disintegrated.

3. Stir in the cilantro and lime juice. Transfer the salsa to a container, cool, cover, and store for up to 3 days in the refrigerator or in the freezer for up to 1 month.

COOKING TIP: Get even more flavor out of this salsa by charring the onion, jalapeños, poblanos, and tomatillos ahead of time. Heat a large dry skillet until it's very hot. Cut the onion in half and place it cut-side down in the skillet along with the whole peppers and tomatillos. Cook until the onion is deeply browned, and the peppers and tomatillos are browned on a few sides. Cool the mixture before dicing and adding it to the slow cooker.

Mango Chutney

Prep time: **10 minutes** / Cook time: **4 hours on low** / Serves: **6 to 8**
Dairy-Free / Gluten-Free / Nut-Free / Vegan

Sweet-and-spicy chutneys are my jam. You can't go wrong with fiery chiles, sweet fruit, and fragrant spices. They go well with bread of all sorts, especially naan, and on top of tangy dairy, such as goat cheese, feta, or full-fat plain yogurt.

4 mangos, peeled, pitted, and diced

2 apples, peeled, cored, and diced

2 red chiles, minced

1 cup sugar

¼ cup lime juice

1 tablespoon minced fresh ginger

2 cinnamon sticks

½ teaspoon ground coriander

¼ teaspoon sea salt

1 teaspoon minced garlic

1. Put the mangos, apples, chiles, sugar, lime juice, ginger, cinnamon sticks, coriander, salt, and garlic in the slow cooker crock. Stir gently to mix.

2. Cover and cook on low for 4 hours.

3. Use the chutney immediately or transfer it to a container, cool, cover, and store for up to 3 days in the refrigerator or in the freezer for up to 1 month.

VARIATION TIP: This chutney is also tasty with Fuyu persimmons (the kind that's most common in the grocery store). Replace the mangos and apples with 12 persimmons, cored and diced. No need to peel.

Mulled Cider

Prep time: **10 minutes** / Cook time: **3 to 4 hours on low** / Serves: **6 to 8**
Dairy-Free / Gluten-Free / Nut-Free / Vegan

Even if I didn't enjoy a steaming mug of hot cider, it would be worth it to prepare it in my slow cooker. It fills the house with all of the delicious aromas of the fall and winter seasons—citrus, cinnamon, cloves, and ginger. See the tip following the recipe for a cocktail version, perfect to serve at a holiday party.

8 cups unfiltered
  apple cider
2 oranges, cut into slices
¼ cup brown sugar
2 cinnamon sticks
1 tablespoon whole cloves
1-inch piece fresh ginger,
  cut into thin rounds

1. Put the apple cider, orange slices, brown sugar, cinnamon sticks, cloves, and ginger in the slow cooker crock. Stir to mix.

2. Cover and cook on low for 3 to 4 hours, until it reaches your desired intensity of flavor.

VARIATION TIP: Spike the mulled cider with 1½ cups of bourbon just before serving for a spirited cocktail version.

Measurement Conversions

Volume Equivalents (Liquid)

US STANDARD	US STANDARD (OUNCES)	METRIC (APPROXIMATE)
2 tablespoons	1 fl. oz.	30 mL
¼ cup	2 fl. oz.	60 mL
½ cup	4 fl. oz.	120 mL
1 cup	8 fl. oz.	240 mL
1½ cups	12 fl. oz.	355 mL
2 cups or 1 pint	16 fl. oz.	475 mL
4 cups or 1 quart	32 fl. oz.	1 L
1 gallon or 4 quarts	128 fl. oz.	4 L

Oven Temperatures

FAHRENHEIT	CELSIUS (APPROXIMATE)
250°F	120°C
300°F	150°C
325°F	165°C
350°F	180°C
375°F	190°C
400°F	200°C
425°F	220°C
450°F	230°C

Volume Equivalents (Dry)

US STANDARD	METRIC (APPROXIMATE)
⅛ teaspoon	0.5 mL
¼ teaspoon	1 mL
½ teaspoon	2 mL
¾ teaspoon	4 mL
1 teaspoon	5 mL
1 tablespoon	15 mL
¼ cup	59 mL
⅓ cup	79 mL
½ cup	118 mL
⅔ cup	156 mL
¾ cup	177 mL
1 cup	235 mL
2 cups or 1 pint	475 mL
3 cups	700 mL
4 cups or 1 quart	1 L

Weight Equivalents

US STANDARD	METRIC (APPROXIMATE)
½ ounce	15 g
1 ounce	30 g
2 ounces	60 g
4 ounces	115 g
8 ounces	225 g
12 ounces	340 g
16 ounces or 1 pound	455 g

References

Bean Institute. "Cooking Beans in the Slow Cooker." Accessed October 31, 2020. BeanInstitute.com/cooking-beans-in-the-slow-cooker.

Benlafquih, Christine. "The Moroccan Tagine." *The Spruce Eats*. Last modified June 18, 2019. TheSpruceEats.com/the-moroccan-tagine-2394748.

Brown, Alton. "The Fungal Saute." *Food Network*. Accessed November 29, 2020. FoodNetwork.com/recipes/alton-brown/the-fungal-saute-recipe-1950881.

Child, Julia, Louisette Bertholle, and Simone Beck. *Mastering the Art of French Cooking*. New York: Knopf, 2001.

Favreau, Jon, dir. *Chef*. Encino, CA: Aldamisa Entertainment, 2014.

Goldfield, Hannah. "You Think You Know Umami." *The New Yorker*. March 19, 2015. NewYorker.com/culture/culture-desk/you-think-you-know-umami.

Nosrat, Samin. *Salt, Fat, Acid, Heat*. New York: Simon & Schuster, 2017.

Royal Craft Wood. "What Type of Cutting Board Is the Best? Bamboo Cutting Board vs Plastic: Who Is the Winner?" September 26, 2018. RoyalCraftWood.com/bamboo-cutting-board-vs-plastic-who-is-the-winner.

United States Department of Agriculture Food Safety and Inspection Service. "'Danger Zone' (40°F–140 °F)." Last modified June 28, 2017. FSIS.USDA.gov/wps/portal/fsis/topics/food-safety-education/get-answers/food-safety-fact-sheets/safe-food-handling/danger-zone-40-f-140-f.

Uribarri, Jaime, Sandra Woodruff, Susan Goodman, Weijing Cai, Xue Chen, Renata Pyzik, Angie Yong, Gary E. Striker, and Helen Vlassara. "Advanced Glycation End Products in Foods and a Practical Guide to Their Reduction in the Diet." *Journal of the American Dietetic Association* 110, no. 6 (2010): 911–16.e12. DOI.org/10.1016/j.jada.2010.03.018.

Index

Acknowledgments

I am so grateful to my family for their patience as I navigated writing a book while we were all on lockdown. Your kindness and cooperative spirit have been wonderful. Also, many thanks to the editorial team at Callisto Media, especially Kelly Koester who walked through this entire manuscript with me step-by-step. I'm grateful for my ongoing relationship with Callisto and the opportunity to share amazing recipes with an even wider audience.

About the Author

 Pamela Ellgen is the author of more than a dozen cookbooks, including *Simple Superfood Soups* and *Healthy Slow Cooker Cookbook for Two*. She lives in Southern California with her husband, two boys, and a lovable goldendoodle puppy named June. When Pamela's not in the kitchen whipping up inspiring new recipes, you can find her at the beach with a surfboard and coconut water.

CPSIA information can be obtained
at www.ICGtesting.com
Printed in the USA
JSHW050032200421
13744JS00006B/56